ATTACHMENT THEORY

Learn How to Build Beautiful Relationships in your Life that Will Last For Ever

By

AMANDA HOPE

TABLE OF CONTENTS

INTRODUCTION

Love that lasts is the result of partners embedding themselves in each other's brains in a positive way. Memory circuits and pleasure get all wound up together so that the other person becomes integral to the very structure of your brain, and you become part of the structure of theirs.

All romantic relationships go up and down, and they are all able to adapt and evolve with your partner. But, if your relationship starts or you're together for years, you should take steps to create a healthy relationship. Even if you have endured several relationships that have been failing or have fought before rekindling the flames of passion in your current relationship, you will learn to remain connected, to come true and enjoy lasting happiness.

Are you and your hopes shattered in the early stages of a new relationship? Are you concerned that you don't know how to make it last? Today, in and outside of a relationship, there are several variables that can affect its outcome.

One of the best things in life is to be in a committed relationship. Getting a good friend to talk to and kiss and cuddle all the time is pretty cool.

Good people exhibit certain common behaviors. While friendship is great, it is even better to be in a fully committed partnership.

If you are in a new relationship and think you might have found the person you want to be with forever, you might ask if you can do anything to maintain a healthy, happy, and lasting relationship.

No matter how long you were together, there are some basic, simple road rules. It's not always easy to put them into effect, but it's important. Make your relationship stronger and the good things – fun, sex, faith, love – greater than ever before.

In the last few years, you could have heard the word 'attachment' floating around the internet. Attachment theory has something to do with how we interact in our most cherished relationships with the most important people. Think about families, relatives and close friends. Attachment is a feeling of comfort in ourselves, in others and around us in the world. And as so much we learn in our families of birth, we also learn from our caregivers about protection and attachment.

Attachment theory tells us that protection which we learned through attachment is extremely important as it impacts our ability to be healthy. And safe bonds are the keys to heaven! Happy and healthy relationships give meaning to our lives and help us to feel connected and developed throughout the world! Oh, yeah, interesting things to remember! Take a minute to crack it.

WHAT IS ATTACHMENT?

The attachment status of a person is a fundamental determinant of their ties, and this is expressed in the way they feel about themselves and others.

Psychologists Mary Ainsworth and John Bowlby are grateful for becoming MVPs in this area called attachment. The research contributed to what we now know about relationship types-more soon. Ainsworth and Bowlby did this. That is, the way we attach ourselves and why we attach ourselves matter above all else.

Your attachment style defines the kind of relationship you had as a child with your caregiver. When you were sad, exhausted, afraid, or hungry as an infant, either your caregiver was or didn't take care of your needs. If your caregiver meets your needs and you learn how to rely on them, you have a healthy form of attachment. Around 56% of the population have this kind of connection. If your caregiver is incompatible with your needs, you may have apprehension for 20 per cent of the population. And if you neglect or disregard your needs, you will definitely grow an avoiding attachment style: about 23 percent of the population are people with an avoiding attachment style. The least common type of attachment, found in approximately 1 % of the population, is disordered attachments and can occur if harassment or aggression takes place at home.

Attachment Theory describes how we build relationships with others in order to satisfy emotional needs. As infants, our lives rely literally on our caregivers for our needs. These conditions include physical necessities such as food, water, security and emotional needs, YES. Stuff like control of the nervous system, love, warmth and relaxation.

Mostly consistent & dependable care

When a primary caregiver reacts more to these physical and emotional needs in a reliable and consistent manner, we establish what is called a secure attachment style. (The focus is primarily on a word because individuals are not perfect and neither carers are perfect!) Caregivers provide the child with a stable basis or consistent availability. This safe base allows the child to move away to explore the world and then be near for security in the event of fear or risk. Really cool, okay?

An attachment was defined by John Bowlby as "the lasting psychological bond of human beings."

Think of a newborn child. This newly baked child needs another person to take care of its basic needs.

WHY DOES IT MATTER?

It is important because we learn what the important people in our lives expect, beginning with the time we are born. Tell that our parents cannot (or will not) be there for us regularly and effectively. Then we discover that the things we need are not accurate.

We are also beings that render sense. The stories we write about our lives tell us what we believe in other people and what we need. It sends a message if our parents do not have the basics and regularly respond to our needs. Unconsciously this message may also be documented as "we don't want to be taken care of." This is what affects us as we grow up and have adult relationships.

Let's assume, for example, that your partner forgets to keep a small promise. Maybe it doesn't seem much. But it may feel like the misery you had endured when you were left alone too long in your crib by mistake and became terrified.

Does that make sense, yes?

Neurobiologically wired for attachment

This stuff is really important, all of it. As primates, we are related neurobiologically to others. Think about it! Our instinct of communicating with others will overpower our intellect, our capacity or our urge to eat or sleep! This is serious business!

Our style of attachment forms the patterns of conduct we can see in our lives.

How the Attachment Theory Developed

The first attachment theorist in British psychology, John Bowlby, described attachment as a "long psychological bond between human beings." Bowlby was keen to understand the anxiety and depression over separation faced by children when separated from their primary caregivers.

Some of the earliest theories of behavior indicated that attachment was merely a learned behavior. The theories that attachment was merely the product of the child-caregiver feeding relationship. The infant is attached because the caregiver feeds the infant and offers nourishment.

What Bowlby discovered was that even feeding did not alleviate the discomfort of children when they were removed from their primary caregivers. Instead, he noticed that attachment had strong motivational and behavioral trends. When children are afraid, they may seek proximity from the primary caregiver to obtain warmth as well as treatment.

Understanding Attachment

Attachment is an emotional relationship with someone else. Bowlby thought that the earliest interactions between children and their caregivers have a huge impact that persists throughout life. He indicated that attachment would also help keep the child close to the mother and thus improve the chances of survival of the child.

Bowlby saw attachment as a result of democratic processes. Although behavioral attachment theories have indicated that attachment is a learned process, Bowlby and others have suggested that children are born with an innate urge to form attachments to caregivers.

Throughout the literature, children who held close to an attachment figure we're more likely to receive comfort and protection, and thus to survive in adulthood. A motivational system designed to control the attachment was created through the process of natural selection.

So, what makes an attachment successful? Behavioralists believe this attachment behavior was triggered by food, while Bowlby and others found that diet and responsiveness were the principal determinants of attachment.

THE THEME OF ATTACHMENT THEORY

The key concept of attachment theory is the primary caregivers available to help the child develop a sense of protection. The baby understands that the caregiver is dependable, which provides a secure base for the child to explore the world then.

Ainsworth's "Strange Situation"

Psychologist Mary Ainsworth has built significantly on Bowlby's original work in her 1970s studies. Her pioneering research on "Strange Circumstance" showed the strong effects of attachment on behavior. In the study, researchers examined children aged 12 to 18 months reacting to a situation where they were left alone briefly and then re-joined with their mothers.

Ainsworth has identified three key types of attachment on the basis of the answers the researchers have seen: stable attachment, ambivalent-insecure fixation and avoidant-insecure attachment. Subsequently, researchers Main and Solomon (1986), based on their own study, introduced a fourth stylus known as disorganization-insecure attachment.

A variety of studies have supported Ainsworth's attachment styles since that period and have shown that attachment styles also affect habits later in life.

Maternal Deprivation Studies
Early links were also discussed in Harry Harlow's infamous research in the 1950s and 1960s on maternal deprivation and social isolation. Harlow showed in a number of studies how these relations arise and how they have a significant effect on actions and functioning.

Newborn rhesus monks were separated from their mothers in one iteration of their experiment, and they were raised by surrogate mothers. The baby monkeys were put in cages with two mothers of wire monkey. One of the wire monkeys housed a bottle from which the baby monkey could get food while the other wire monkey was covered with a soft terry cloth.

As the children's monks went to the wire mother to get food, they spent most of their days with the soft cloth mother. The baby monkeys would turn to their cloth-covered mother for comfort and security when they were scared.

Harlow's work also showed that early attachments were the product of a caregiver's comfort and treatment instead of just being fed.

THE STAGES OF ATTACHMENT

In a longitudinal study of 60 children, researchers Rudolph Schaffer and Peggy Emerson analyzed the number of connective relationships that infants form. In the first year of life, babies were observed every four weeks and then again at 18 months.

Schaffer and Emerson outlined four distinct phases of attachment in the light of their observations, including:

Pre-Attachment Stage
At birth to 3 months, children are not bound to a single caregiver. The child's indications, such as weeping and fussing, instinctively call the caregiver's attention and baby's positive reactions allow the caregiver to stay near.

Indiscriminate Attachment
Between the six weeks and seven months of age, children begin to demonstrate primary and secondary caregivers preferences. Children gain faith that the caregiver meets their needs. Although children are still receiving treatment from others, they begin to differentiate between families and strangers and react to the primary caregiver more positively.

Discriminate Attachment

At this stage, children between 7 and 11 months of age display a clear attachment and affection for a certain person. They complain when they are separated from the primary figure of attachment (separation anxiety) and start displaying concern for strangers (stranger anxiety).

Multiple Attachments

Children begin to develop strong emotional connections with other caregivers outside the primary connection after around nine months of age. Often the dad, older sisters and grandparents are part of this.

Factors That Influence Attachment

While this method may seem straightforward, certain factors can affect the production and creation of attachments, including:

Opportunity for attachment: Children with no primary care, including those brought up in orphanages, may not build the sense of confidence required to form an attachment.

Quality Care: When caregivers respond rapidly and reliably, children understand that they can rely on others who take care of them, which is the basic basis for attachment. This is a significant aspect.

PATTERNS OF ATTACHMENT

There are four patterns of attachment, including:

Anxious attachment: when a parent leaves, these children become very sad. The unusual type of Anxious attachment affects an estimated 7-15% of American children. These children cannot rely on their primary caregiver to be there if they need them because of poor parental availability.

Avoidant attachment: Children with a preventative relationship tend to avoid parents or caregivers and don't prefer a caregiver over an absolute outsider. This form of attachment can be induced by violent or neglectful caregivers. Children disciplined for relying on a caregiver will learn to stop finding assistance in the future.

Disorganized attachment: These children exhibit a frustrating, disoriented, dazzled, or disturbing combination of behaviors. The parent may avoid or resist. There is possibly a lack of a simple attachment pattern that is related to inconsistent behavior. In these situations, parents may also act as a source of comfort and anxiety, which results in disorderly behavior.

Stable attachment: children who can rely on their caregiver's display sadness in separation and joy in reunification. While the child will be upset, the caregiver is sure to come back. When scared, tightly attached children search for support from caregivers.

The Lasting Impact of Early Attachment

Research indicates that failure to establish healthy attachments early in life may have a detrimental influence on later childhood and lifelong behaviour.9

Oppositional defiant disorder (ODD), behavioral disorder (CD) and post-traumatic stress disorder (PTSD) are also diagnosed with attachment difficulties, likely because of early abuse, neglect, or trauma. Clinicians say that the probability of attachment issues is greater for children who are accepted after age six months.

Although types of attachment in adulthood are not inherently the same as in infancy, the early attachment may seriously affect later relationships. Many who are comfortable in infancy appear to have good self-confidence, positive interpersonal connections, and the willingness to expose themselves to others.

Kids who are firmly attached to mothers appear to develop greater self-esteem and self-sufficiency as they grow older. These children are much more independent, better at school, have good social relations and have less depression and less anxiety.

THE FOUR STYLES OF ATTACHMENT

According to psychologists, adults can adopt four adhesive strategies: secure, anxious, avoidant, and anxious-avoidant.

SECURE ATTACHMENT STYLE

People with secure attachment techniques will express interest and affection easily. They are happy to be alone and alone. They should prioritize their relationships in their lives correctly and tend to draw and adhere to specific boundaries.

Obviously, reliable fasteners make the best romantic partners, family members and even friends. They are able to embrace refusal and continue amid their discomfort, but they can be loyal and compromise when necessary. They have no trouble trusting people with whom they are close and trustworthy.

Research indicates that over 50 % of the population are stable forms of attachment.

ANXIOUS ATTACHMENT STYLE

Often anxious attachment types are depressed and uncertain about their relationships. They need your partner's constant reassurance and love. You have problems being alone or alone. Often, they excel in dysfunctional or abusive relationships. Even if they are next to them, they have trouble trusting people. Their actions can be erratic, inconsistent, and overly emotional and complain of the cold and heartless essence of each other's sex.

This is the girl who calls you in one night 36 times, asking why you haven't called her yet. Or the man who follows his friend to work to make sure that she doesn't sleep with any other guy. Women are more likely than men to be nervous.

AVOIDANT ATTACHMENT STYLE

The avoided forms of attachments are extremely independent, autonomous and often uncomfortable with intimacy. They are dedicated and professionals who can streamline their way out of any intimate situation. You often complain that if people try to get close to it, they feel "crowded" or "suffered." They always have an exit strategy in every relationship. Still. Always. And often they develop their lives to prevent interaction or too much intimate contact.

Theory of attachment: Avoiding form

This is the man who works 80 hours a week and gets angry if he tries to see him more than once on the weekend. Or the girl who dates hundreds of guys over the years but says to them all she doesn't want "serious" and ends up telling them when she gets tired of them eventually. Men are more likely to be avoiding styles than women.

ANXIOUS-AVOIDANT ATTACHMENT STYLE

Anxious-Avoidant: The worst of both worlds is the anxious-avoiding attachment styles (also called the "fearful type"). Concerns are not only terrified of intimacy and engagement, but they also fear and emotionally attack someone who attempts to reach them. Sometimes, courageous people spend most of their time alone and in pain, or in abusive or insecure relationships.

Studies show that only a small proportion of the population identify as anxious-preventative types, and they typically experience a host of other emotional problems in other areas of their lives (e.g. drug abuse, depression, etc.).

Like most psychological profiles, these types are not monolithic, but in fact scalar and somewhat autonomous. According to the book Amir Levie and Rachel Heller, for instance, I scored approximately 75% on the safety scale, 90% on the preventing scale, and 10% on the worrying scale. And I think 3-5 years ago it would have been better and more nervous, but my event has always been completely maxed out (as any of my ex-girlfriends would say to you).

The point is, you can demonstrate more than one technique at different frequencies, depending on the situation. Everyone has a winning strategy, however. So "stable" types continue to have some evasive or nervous behaviors, "anxious" types are sometimes healthy. This isn't anything or nothing. Anxious styles and avoiding forms also get a certain amount on a safe scale. However, anxiety preventers are high in both anxious and avoiding forms and low on a healthy scale.

HOW ATTACHMENT STYLES ARE FORMED

As I have said before, our relationship as adults depends on how we relate to our parents (or one parent / primary caregiver) as young children. This is our first and important relationship in our lives as helpless little infants, which inevitably sets the "blueprint" for how we view all our relationships as we age.

We use this relation as we age into late infancy and adolescence when we normally start developing substantial relationships beyond our close relationship with our parent(s). Our community of peers plays an expanded role in our lives as we learn how to communicate with others. These interactions further affect our attachment style, as we ultimately interact with other people, who in turn influence our attachment style.

So, while your early interactions with your parent(s) affect your relationship with others considerably, this is not the only factor that decides your attachment style (which is a major one, though) and your attachment style can change over time (more about it later).

Generally speaking, however, children who consistently meet their needs and receive sufficient amounts of love and affection build a healthy connection in their childhood. You feel confident among your fellow workers but are still relaxed with your weaknesses. They have good, clear boundaries, can connect well in their relationships with their desires and are not afraid to leave a bad person when they feel they must.

In infancy, nervous attachment techniques are formed by children receiving uncertain affection and care. They normally see their colleagues favorably, but they see themselves negatively. Their romantic relationships are often too idealized and depend too heavily on them for self-esteem.

Avoidance attachment approach is established in children who only meet some of their needs while the rest is overlooked (e.g., they are routinely fed but are not kept sufficiently). You also have a negative opinion of others but a positive view of yourself. They didn't focus too much on their romantic relationships and feel like they can't emotionally help others.

Styles of anxiety-preventing grow out of dysfunctional or horribly incompetent infancy. They also have trouble communicating with their peers. In romantic relationships, they pursue both intimacy and freedom, often simultaneously, which, you might imagine, leads to some pretty messy, unstable ties.

ADULT ATTACHMENT STYLES AND RELATIONSHIP CONFIGURATIONS

Different forms of attachments tend to configure themselves in interpersonal ties inevitably. Safe styles are both nervous and avoidant for dating (or managing depending on your perspective). They are relaxed enough to give worried types all the reassurance they need and to give avoiding types of the room that they need without feeling threatened.

Sorrowful and evasive people often end up in ties with each other more often than in relationships with each other. Which may seem counter-intuitive, but behind the chaos is order. Avoiding forms are so good at putting others off that often it is

23

only the concerned kinds who are willing to stay around and try to get them available.

For example, a man who is avoiding may successfully shirk the drive of a secure woman for more privacy. Then the healthy woman acknowledges the denial and moves on. But a worried woman is decided only by a man who drives her away. For weeks or months, she will call him before he eventually yields and commits him to it. This gives the avoidant the reassurance that he can act freely and that the nervous woman will wait for him.

They also create some degree of unstable balance when they fall into a chaser-chasee pattern that is the two roles that anxious and avoidant styles have to play to be comfortable with intimacy.

Attachment Theory: Anxious-avoidant
Anxious avoiders either date each other or are the less stable of anxious types or evasive types. These are very messy, if not abusive or incompetent relationships.

All this is that insecurity seeks insecurity and protection, even if these insecurities are not exactly the same. To put it simply, anyone who has contacted me over the years with the concern that all people they meet are incompetent, or have problems of confidence, or vulnerable and manipulative.

WHAT'S YOUR ATTACHMENT STYLE?

Note: a true friend story bellow

I always think about and laugh at all the stuff that nobody said we'd have to find as adults (more like face palm, roll my eyes, sigh/snort dramatically as loud as I can). There are so many things that we have never been taught, but I assume it is because our parents did not even have a clue. And many certainly don't, sadly.

Disclaimer: I strongly believe that for what they know, all parents do their best they can. In one way or another, our parents fucked us all. Typically, as we operate in adulthood, the Holy Moment in which we see them as infants, their parents, is when we actually comprehend it and can meet them where they stand. In another post, I'll get to that, back to us for now.

We live in this time and space where we have so much knowledge. We are able to develop the ability to live full of abundance, emotional awareness/intellect, personal development and good personal, social, professional and particularly romantic relationships: we never did our parents and their predecessors. I say "most of all," because I think that is where most of us like we're struggling the hardest, or getting it wrong. But we have not to. So, we do not have to.

We have complete access to resources at all times that will teach us the development of skills: blogs, podcasts and books you can buy from your local library. Anything for free. Now even therapists/coaches are open, slipping, and use only text or e-mail to make it accessible for all. No reason for not knowing how to grow and master ourselves. When I sit here Sunday morning, with my cat snuggling against my right hip, watching Varsity Blues for what seems the 726th time, still in awe at Eliud Kipchoge's sub-2 marathon that he eventually won (I might have shrunk on it yesterday), all I have thought about is to be delivered. Let your blockers blue and get cozy, that's a long one.

I read a book in 2017 that always changed the way I treated interpersonal relations. After listening to the news, Amir Levine, M.D. And I gave it a shot, Rachel S. F. Heller, M.A. I was doing too much work on myself at that time, what was another piece of education? In about three days, I finished it, which is fast for me, even with a book worm.

Some Sundays ago, after meeting a thirty-something lady who opened her life a little, I instantly felt like that. Before my wheels spun and my reds waved vigorously in my mind (accompanied by sirens, flashing stop signs and bright yellow warning tape, I was the only one to see it right now). I walked over and pulled Connected to my bookshelf, from its place in my area of personal growth. I gave her the book and, when she finished it, I told her to pass it on to someone else who could find it useful.

Research shows (I'm glad to say that now that I'm doing more research at school) that the same factors that establish an emotional relationship between parents and children later decide how this boy, now an adult, approaches romantic interrelationships. Fucked up, right? Fucked up, right?

Theorist John Bowlby was the first person, who built upon this research in the seventies, to study attachment types before psychologist Mary Ainsworth. There are so many studies today which have really delved into this phenomenon. Trigger the appendices.

The first attachments are developed in early childhood and in emotional/romantic connections over developmental years until they emerge in adulthood. If you think that we're not having our children in unhealed adult bodies, think again. Think again. Only get to styles. Let's get to styles.

The first type of attachment is the worried attachment. Persons with nervous relationships are in the relationship just like this: nervous. There are people who are constantly on the verge of being betrayed or cheated by their partner. Usually, they are nervous, they have annoying feelings, they're jealous, and they're called "clingy." They want to be together all the time; a sense of codependence and connection exists. If your desires are not met, you might do anything to make your partner jealous. Ironically, they often appear to pick partners that fill up this exact definition, the avoidant. They have relationships like a cat and mouse game, which are generally unstable. (We'll get to the avoidant group soon.)

Anxious connections are formed when the parent-child relationship is inconsistent (remember this word!). The child did not meet its emotional needs, and it should have been more important for the parent to satisfy itself.

This form of incompatibility then emerges as an anxious attachment in adulthood. The infant is the adult who pursues an intimate bond, normally with someone who is emotionally unavailable / uniform as the caregiver has been.

CUE THE AVOIDANT PARTNER.

In adulthood, the Avoidant attachment style is offered to those who reject. In romantic relationships this person is often inaccessible emotionally, he prevents himself from getting too close to someone, considers his partners "clingy" (although they do not, of course, give them a reason to be) and he prefers to handle emotions himself (shut down mode) or shake his feelings off. Author Mark Manson simply describes it in a meaningful way.

"This is the man who works 80 hours a week and gets irritated if the dates of the women want to see him on the weekend more than once. They still have an escape plan in any relationship. Still. Still. And often they develop their lifestyles to escape interaction ...

These people have a grandiose view of themselves or seem to have high respect for themselves while they look at others as if they are superior. This masks the harsh reality: they have low self-esteem and are extremely fragile. They will encircle themselves with people who will validate their own self-image, and they will come out, discard and have a solution ready in no time when it ends. You will find them in a relationship physically but never fully committed.

Sound like you know someone? The narcissist, yes. Yes. I'm going to get to narcs in another story too, as I had my run-ins one or two times in my day. It was a great time (I hope you felt my sarcasm and my attitude incredibly dry).

The reason why anxieties and evaders always come together is that the safe person takes the L and keeps it going while the avoidant pushes away a safe person. The anxious person will continue to work until the evader eventually "bids," who are the anxious children who, as a child, may have had to ask for attention and now are nervous, hungry adults. It also confirms that he (we'll use "he" because most avoiders are male) can act as he wants. He doesn't have to change: obviously, the nervous person won't go anywhere. The participants call this "passion," people call it insanity in their own minds. Insecurity is often magnetized into insecurity.

The preventative attachment is established in infancy when only certain needs of the infant are met. For example, in that context, the infant is fed, bathed and taken care of but is not kept enough, rendered "cry it out," told to stop crying, and became independent early on. (This reminds me how my mum told me, 'I could leave you all day on your own in your playpen, you're perfect.' While I'm ferociously independent, I understand it's NOT a good thing.)

Finally, our friends are safely linked. Where do we aspire to be, are stable attachments? These grownups are the ones with good self-esteem, they are secure in whom they are and okay with their flaws, they seek social support, they have no issues alone, they are empathetic adults, and they are assured that end-of-life relationships are not meaningless or perceived to be evil.

When children are regularly taken care of by their caregivers, stable attachments are created. Their basic needs and their emotional needs are fulfilled. Besides the parents, they also have daily love and affection from others. That's what builds the confidence of the kid.

There we have it, quick to understand POV from my "watered down." Mind-blowing, isn't it, to see how much our adult lives are determined by the 0–12 Mondays and the selection of children? If you inquire if you can change your type of attachment, the simple answer is yes.

Not all types of adult attachment are childhood-based, but most of them. Life encounters can also alter the type of attachment. I was also nervous and preventative until I was the firmly attached person I am today again.

HOW YOUR ATTACHMENT STYLE IMPACTS YOUR RELATIONSHIP

Our attachment style affects everything from our selection of partners to how well our relationships advance and, unfortunately, how they finish. Therefore, understanding our attachment pattern will enable us to recognize our strengths and weaknessesin our relationship. An attachment pattern is established in early infancy attachments and remains a working model for adult relationships.

This attachment model affects how each and every one of us responds to our needs and how we accomplish them. When there is a stable pattern of attachment, a person is confident and self-sufficient and can communicate easily with other people, satisfying both his and his own needs. When a person chooses a partner that matches the pattern of maladaptation, though, he or she usually chooses someone who isn't the perfect choice to make him or her happy.

For example, the person who has a working model of anxious/consuming attachment feels that you have to be with your partner all the time and be encouraged to get close to someone and meet your needs. They choose someone who is alone and hard to communicate with to support this perception of reality. The individual with a working model of an evasive attachment appears to be far away because its philosophy is that the way to satisfy your needs is to behave like you do not have it. Then he or she prefers someone more possessive or unnecessarily vigilant.

In a way, we have found collaborators to validate our models. If we have established an insecure pattern of attachment, we will project or attempt to replicate similar patterns of relationships with adults, even if these patterns damage us and are not in our own self-interest.

Dr Phillip Shaver and Dr Cindy Hazan found that 60% of the individuals have a secure attachment while 20% have an evasive attachment, and 20% have an anxious attachment in their study. What does it mean? There are questions to help you determine your attachment style and how it affects your relationships.

You will begin to define your own relationship by learning about the four attachment patterns in adults and how they affect couples.

Stable attachment – Adults who are safely attached appear to be more fulfilled. Children with a secure attachment consider their parent as a safe base from which to explore the world independently. A healthy adult has the same relationship with his romantic partner and feels secure and connected, allowing himself and his partner to move freely.

When your partner feels sad, stable adults offer support. You also go to your partner for support if you feel depressed yourself. Their link appears to be honest, open and fair, with both individuals feeling independent yet loving one another. Stable couples do not tend to engage in what my father, psychologist Robert Firestone, describes as a "fantasy bond," a binding illusion that generates a false sense of security. In a fantasy relationship, a few forget the true love for a more normal, emotionally disrupted form of interaction.

Concerned attachment – In contrast to securely attached pairs, people with anxious attachment are starting to develop fantasy links. They also feel emotional hunger rather than feeling true love or confidence for their partner. They also attempt to rescue or complete their partner. While they seek a sense of security by binding themselves to their partner, they take actions that drive their partner away.

While people with anxiety behave instinctively or dangerous, their actions exacerbate their own fears more often than not. When you feel unsure of your partner's sentiments and uncertain about your relationship, you are often clinging, demanding or possessive to your partner. They may also view their partner's independent behavior as confirmation of their fears. For example, if your partner begins to socialize more with friends, you may say, "See? He just doesn't love me. That means he'll leave me. He will leave me. I haven't been able to believe him.

Discarding Avoidant attachment – People with a discarding, rejecting attachment tend to separate themselves emotionally from their partner. They will look for autonomy and feel pseudo-independent, taking on the role of parenting. Often, they are focused on themselves and can take excessive care of their creature comfort.

Pseudo-independence is an illusion since every human being requires a relationship. Nonetheless, people with a gross evasive attachment tend to lead more inner lives, denying and detaching themselves quickly from their loved ones. They often have a psychological buffer and an internal shutdown. Even in heated or emotional circumstances, they may turn their feelings off and not respond. For example, they would reply by saying "I don't care," if their partner were depressed and threatened to leave them.

Fearful Obvious Attachment – A person whose evil attachment is afraid of being too near or too far from others' lives in an Anxious state. They try to keep their feelings in check, but they cannot. You can't just suppress your fear or hide your emotions. They are often overwhelmed by their emotions and sometimes suffer from emotional storms. In their moods, they appear to be mixed or volatile. You see their relationships from the working paradigm that you must go to others to fulfil your needs, but they will harm you if you get close to them. In other words, the person they want is the same person they are scared to get next to. As a result, they don't have a coordinated plan to meet their needs.

As adults, these people appear to experience several peaks and lows in tumultuous or unstable relationships. They also fear rejection but often struggle with intimacy. You will stick to your partner if you feel rejected, and you may feel stuck when you are near. The time between them and their partner always seems to be off. An individual with a terrible evader can even experience an abusive relationship.

Your relationship with a parent or an early caregiver does not need to describe the ways to connect to the loved ones in your adult life. If you become acquainted with your type of attachment, you will find out how you protect yourself from being near and emotionally involved and work for a healthy attachment.

By selecting a partner in a secure attachment style, you can test your defenses and establish yourself in this relationship. Therapy can also help to alter patterns of maladaptive behavior. By knowing your attachment style, you and your partner will question the insecurities and fears reinforced by your old working habits and build new attachment styles for maintaining a fulfilling, loving relationship.

IDENTIFY YOUR ATTACHMENT STYLE AND FIND SOMEONE WHO FITS YOURS

Some relationships have compatible forms of attachment. Others aren't so fortunate. When anyone comes up with a new type of attachment, it can lead to all sorts of tension in the relationship. One such disagreement may be about time. For instance, attachment theory explains why some people expect their partners to spend their entire free time. But some don't want or have to spend too much time with their friends. This disparity will make two people struggle as they try to compromise on how much time they have to spend in relationships.

Changing your attachment style is a long and difficult process.

You may always attempt to change your specific style of attachment, but this is a long and complicated process. According to attachment theory, when we are little girls, we build our attachment style. Typically, it is focused on our relationship with our parents.

Instead, we will discuss the various forms of attachments and which combinations are best for relationships. You can find a partner who suits your needs if you can recognize your exact relationship style. Naturally, this is the optimal condition. But if your partnership is already in place and your attachment combination isn't so good, don't worry! You and your significant others still have hope.

Each combination of attachments has a different perspective on the relationship.

Positive Outlook

If one person has a stable style of attachment, the relationship has a positive perspective. Attachment theory teaches us that the individual with a stable attachment style will affirm the concerns of his partner. You can also help your less stable partner conquer your vulnerability.

Challenging Outlook

The anxious + anxious combination is challenging. People with this attachment style can interpret minor emotional and behavioral shifts. This perceptive capacity and their nervous vulnerability lead to conclusions. In short, two unsure, nervous people may have a relationship that is full of drama, resentment and disagreements. The same applies to the dangerous and disorganized mix.

Suppose one evasive pair up with another evasive, little contact will be established, which might seem good at the start, as both are not demanding. But as time passes, the bond becomes weaker, and the relationship is hard to maintain.

Toxic Combination

If the two relationship types are nervous and evasive, things would be rough. You should probably brace yourself mentally for the kind of problems which this combination might bring to your life. Think again if you think about getting into this relationship.

Interestingly, these two kinds of attachments are also mixed. Since they closely complement each other. A nervous person is afraid to lose his partner, and so they wait until the apparent person agrees to participate in the relationship. This combination validates the actions of the avoidant.

As the unsecured and disorganized style mixes the anxious sort and the avoiding kind, it will be a tragedy for the avoiding sort when the anxious side comes up. When the evasive side arises, tensions occur with the nervous sort. That is why insecurity+ insecure disorganization + insecure disorganization+ insecure disorder is not likely to function.

BE HONEST WITH YOURSELF TO IDENTIFY YOUR ATTACHMENT STYLE.

You must first find someone to match your attachment style. Think of how you respond to what your partner does.

Can you waste half an hour thinking about what could have gone wrong if they tell you they're calling at 6:00 pm, and they don't call before 6:30 pm? Are you starting to feel insecure or feeling that you were possibly abandoned? You undoubtedly have been known to poutor start fights with your partner, be honest with yourself. Does it sound familiar? You're probably an insecure, nervous person.

Think about how you feel after spending a lot of time with others. Do you need time for yourself? Or maybe you may feel like you are going to lose your identity or your freedom in a long-term relationship. If this sounds like you, you may have an unstable form of preventative connection.

OBSERVE YOUR PARTNER'S BEHAVIOR TO FIND OUT THEIR ATTACHMENT STYLE.

It may seem harder to recognize the style of the attachment of your others, but it is not impossible. You do not know exactly how they feel, but you can watch their behavior. Consider how they respond to your concerns. What do they mean, if you have had a rough day and you come home complaining about it? Do you think you don't know if they're really not interested? You may have an insecure method of preventing attachment.

What happens if you are late on a date? If just 3 minutes later, they send a text to ask if you still come, it might be an anxious sort.

There is no ideal relationship, and definitely, no relationship is expected to fail because of attachment styles. However, you will make great progress to ensure your future happiness together by knowing your person and the style of attachment of your partner.

YOUR PARENTS SIGNIFICANTLY INFLUENCE ATTACHMENT STYLE

I hate to say, but your parents have a big hand in how you relate to your romantic partners, select them and connect them. All this began with a fascinating experiment by John Bowlby and Mary Ainsworth in the 1960s. Bowlby and Ainsworth passed the so-called "Strange Circumstance" examination for children and parents.

The Strange Situation:

Imagine that you were put into a big room as a kid. Your mother is moving in. Your mother does not take part in your space discovery. A foreigner comes into the room, talks to your mother and then comes to you. Your mother leaves the room quietly.

How are you reacting?

Finally, your mom returns.

Researchers detect these activities during this exercise:

When the kid explores the room and spends the whole time with the new toys.

What does the child do when its parent disappears.

How the kid interacts with an alien alone.

What does the kid do when the parent comes back?

Depending on how the child responds, the four types of attachment are grouped into four groups that reflect the parent attachment. Researchers conclude that throughout your life, you can retain these relationship patterns and replicate them with families, children and friends.

WHAT'S YOUR PARTNER'S ATTACHMENT STYLE?

What is the relationship style of your partner? There are four adult attachment styles: stable, anxious-presumed, dismissive-avoidant, and afraid-avoidant, based on the work of Bartholomew, Horowitz, etc. Most people have varying degrees of four attachment types that can shift over time.

Below are some of the most influential features of each romantic attachment style

"It's very easy for me to get closer to others in emotion. I'm happy depending on others and depending on me. I don't have fears or other people don't like me."

— Horowitz and Bartholomaios

Those with a good stable attachment style frequently show at least a few of the following:

Higher emotional awareness. Capable of effectively and constructively conveying feelings.

Able to submit and receive safe interpersonal expressions.

May draw safe, sufficient and fair boundaries if necessary.

Feel happy to be alone or with a friend.

The tendency to have a clear understanding of ties and personal experiences.

More likely to deal with relationship issues in advance. Discuss problems to fix problems instead of bullying others.

Resilience to the breakdown of relationships. Able to grieve, learn and step on.

People with a safe style of attachment are not fine. They too, like everyone else, have ups and downs and can get angry if provoked. However, their overall balanced approach to relationships makes this the healthiest of the four types of interaction for adults.

ANXIOUS-PREOCCUPIED ATTACHMENT STYLE

"I want to be completely intimate emotionally with others, but I sometimes find others hesitant to be as close as I want. I'm unhappy without strong connections, but I often worry that people don't trust me as much as I trust them."

— Horowitz RQ and Bartholomew

Those whose style of attachment is intense and nervous tend to exhibit at least some of the following characteristics on a regular basis:

Inclined to feel more anxious and less confident about relationships in general, particularly romantic ones.

Inclined to have multiple stressors in actual and imagined relationships. These stressors can occur through a range of possible problems such as neediness, possibilities, anxiety, power, mood shifting, oversensitivity, obsessiveness, etc.

Unwilling to give others the advantage of the doubt, tend towards unconscious negative thinking when reading the thoughts, words and acts of others.

Continuous love stroking and encouragement are needed to feel comfortable and accepted. Responds negatively if daily positive reinforcement is not given.

Drama focused. Drama focused. Work continuously on (sometimes inventing) topics in order to obtain affirmation, reassurance and acceptance. Some feel more relaxed than calm and happy with stormy relationships.

I don't like to be without company. The war is by itself.

An emotionally tumultuous relationship in the past.

DISMISSIVE-AVOIDANT ATTACHMENT STYLE

It is very necessary that I feel safe and self-sufficient, and I tend not to rely on others or make others rely on me." "I am fine without close interpersonal relationships.

— Horowitz and Bartholomaios

Those with a clear dismissive-avoidant connection style appear to exhibit at least some of the following characteristics frequently:

Extremely automated and automated. Behaviorally and emotionally independent.

Stop real intimacy that makes one insecure and can bind the evasive to emotional obligations.

Physically and mentally, want independence ("nobody puts a neck on me." Any who come too close drive away ("I need space to breathe")

Other life interests often outweigh romantic relationships, such as employment, social life, projects and personal ambitions, travel, fun, etc. The partner is often omitted or has only a limited role in these cases.

Many have trouble with communication. Some people tend to be alone instead of calming down. Particularly in committed partnerships, autonomy is more critical than anything.

May have a lot of expertise, but few very close relationships.

Which may be passive and/or narcissistic.

FEARFUL-AVOIDANT ATTACHMENT STYLE

I want emotionally close connections, but it is difficult for me to trust others fully or to depend on them. I sometimes fear I'll be hurt if I allow myself to get too close to others.

— Horowitz and Bartholomaios

Those with a heavy Fearful-Avoidant Attachment Style appear to convey at least any of the following frequently:

Often related to life experiences with great challenges, including grief, alienation and violence.

Wish, but at the same time avoid intimacy. A lot of internal strife.

Struggle with faith and belief in others.

Fear of death in romantic, intimate circumstances, physically and/or emotionally.

Similar to the anxiously worrying form, suspecting the thoughts, words and acts of others.

Like the decay-evitable style, it keeps people away and has few truly intimate ties.

As already mentioned, most people have different degrees of the four attachment forms, which can change over time.

While primarily Stable Attachment Styles tend to be strong partners, they can also work effectively with those who are primarily the other three styles. Self-consciousness, mutual interest, shared desire to learn and the ability to seek professional assistance when appropriate are essential factors in favor of healthy relationships. However, the absence of these elements can lead to problems of relationship incompatibility.

HOW TO TELL SOMEONE'S ATTACHMENT STYLE ON A FIRST DATE

Hundreds of recent research worldwide suggest that we have a type of attachment that demonstrates how we have relationships with parents and other caregivers as a result of core emotions that we have developed in early infancy. There are three main types of attachment — stable, anxious and avoidable — and although the couples of some attachment styles perform exceptionally well, others can be disastrous. You can learn your own attachment style with a simple quiz, but what about the people you want to date?

Although there is no safe way to know the attachment style of anyone else at a glance, essential hints exist — some of them are also taken on the very first day. After years of study into the current attachment, I have identified the three signs to recognize the type of attachment of an individual at the first meeting:

1. The structure of early conversations.

A first date is basically a chat, and if you try to understand something a person wants to do with others, that is a good thing. Listen carefully, and you will also gather signs showing whether your date is safe (mostly trustful and intimate), preventative (pulling away from separate relationships) or nervous (crowding intimacy and continuous reassurance).

People with evasive forms of attachment can be easily identified from how they communicate in these early interactions: they cannot speak about feelings easily, says Harry Reis, PhD, professor of psychology at Rochester University. Rather, you prefer to concentrate on what you do, your careers, your favorite television shows and other things without getting too personal or insightful.

In the meanwhile, people with a healthy type of relationship will be much more open and flexible about what they are talking about. "In a first conversation, safe people would be comfortable, fun to talk to, easy company."

Dr Reis warns that it can be difficult to say a safe person just from an initial conversation. This is because a nervous person – who is afraid of refusing and would like to do so – will sometimes be funny and display interest in the other person. In other words, they can be as optimistic and engaging as we would expect a healthy person to be, but for another reason they do.

"Most concerned people don't really worry about the other guy," says Dr Reis. "It's like the Bette Midler line, 'It is enough for me. Let's speak to you. What do you think about me?' That's a nervous person talking." 'Well, I'm anxious to talk to you.

Consider the additional first-date hints below to help decide whether your date is healthy or nervous.

2. How much a person self-discloses.
It is unlikely that avoidants would talk much about their inner selves, especially with a virtual stranger. Overall, they can show nothing and remind you, knowingly or not, that they don't even need a partner.

Anxious people appear to divulge too soon — before the other person is ready for closeness. This desire to make yourself known may represent your need to quickly find knowledge, to manage your own anxiety and to feel an interpersonal link before something has been done. The consequence is that they might be vulnerable and daunting.

And healthy people? And clean? They will get to the spot of "Goldilocks." Not too much, not too little, but just right. The stress is likely to be well handled and generally cheerful.

3. Personal dating history.
Safe people in the world tend to be relaxed and happy, whether in a relationship or not. If you discover through conversation that over the years your date has had many serious relationships, but has spent a substantial amount of time without a

relationship, it can be a sign of a person having a stable connection.

Concerned individuals, however, because they long for love and without a partner, feel emotionally incomplete are often part of a series of continuous relationships since their early teens. They can convey intense, unresolved feelings, like holding on to anger or still wearing a torch while talking to the former partners.

In comparison, it may be a sign of indifference if your date is early or mid-adult and is never in a serious relationship. One indication would be if this same person did not seem to have even one or two close friends while listing a broad circle of acquaintances.

WHICH ATTACHMENT STYLES MAKE GOOD MATCHES?

Congratulations, if you are healthy. Attachment research shows that you can have a strong relationship with any form of attachment. You will lead to a stable relationship if you match another healthy individual. If you match an avoidant or nervous person, you can add the relationship intimacy by knowing the attachment needs of your partner and over time, you can encourage your partner to become more private. That is why avoiding, and nervous people would do their best with a safe partner. "You are five steps ahead if you can find anyone safe."

An anxious match can work, but this combination can also lead to partners becoming heavily dependent. It is good to be aware of this, so you can talk about the problem and try to get it right.

An avoidant match can also work, but if the pair reaches the rough patch, both parties might just drop the partnership rather than stick around to work on it.

The match to most of them hold away? That would be anxious – preventative. Every person needs different degrees of intimacy in this combination: the anxious person tries to close while the avoider pulls away. When these requirements are not met, they have different ways of reacting and thus build a vicious cycle that further strains the relationship.

But note: no combination is lost.

There is no combination of attachment styles which definitely cannot function. Also, for the most problem-free variations, a stable and fulfilling partnership is possible when both parties understand how their styles of attachments affect them.

THE ANXIOUS ATTACHMENT STYLE

The baby caregiver relationship is important for the development and comprehension of the world of a baby.

Babies and young children rely on caregivers and learn early social skills by watching the reaction of their caregivers to them and others. They also learn early social skills.

The way a caregiver communicates with a baby or young child will influence the child's style of attachment.

Anxious fasteners are one of four types of fasteners. People with anxiety can have trouble feeling comfortable in relationships. As young children, when a caregiver leaves, they can cling to caregivers or become inconsolable.

As an adult, they can be susceptible to envy or other relationship vulnerability. Anxious attachment can also be called nervous attachment.

UNDERSTANDING ANXIOUS ATTACHMENT

Human beings are born with strong instincts for survival. One of the most important is that a child cannot live alone and relies solely on the adult for nurturance and security. Babies have an inherent desire to ensure that a parent, caregiver or other important person meets their basic needs in their lives. Different children develop different strategies to do this depending on their social state and level of treatment. Annexe theory is the study of this basic instinct, and researchers have grouped diverse strategies into four categories of annexation patterns: secure annexation and two types of unsafe annexation, avoiding attachments and nervous attachment. The fourth type of attachment, called disorganized attachment, arises when no organized strategy is established.

Attachment researchers have established tuning as critical in attachment formation. Attunement means to be in harmony; to be conscious and sensitive to others. Emotional equilibrium requires first equilibrium with oneself, then another and eventually circumstances. Configuration and attachment are linked in that an adult, who is present, compatible and attentive to a child's needs, creates a healthy connection for a child starting in childhood. This harmonization offers a stable framework for the child to explore the world.

A lack of harmony or misunderstanding by a parent or parent leads to an unstable connection in the relationship with their child. I talk about an avoiding pattern of attachment when parents are cold, emotionally unavailable and remote, and children then try to shut down their understanding of their primary needs. This article discusses how an Anxious/anxious relationship forms during infancy and affects adults.

WHAT IS AMBIVALENT/ANXIOUS ATTACHMENT?

Many parents and/or caregivers are inconsistent with their children. Attachment researchers explain the actions of such adults and how they often cultivate, balance and effectively react to their child's distress while they are disruptive, insensitive or emotionally inaccessible at other times. When parents vacillate, their children become confused and anxious, and they do not know what kind of treatment to receive. These children often feel suspicious of their parents, but they are clinging and desperate. You know that the easiest way to fulfil your needs is to stick to your attachment figure. These kids areanxious about their uncertain parent.

WHAT BEHAVIORS ARE ASSOCIATED WITH AN ANXIOUS ATTACHMENT PATTERN?

Children with an Anxious/anxious attachment pattern appear to attach themselves to their attachment figures and often behave desperately. Mary Ainsworth, who examined child's attachment patterns for 12 to 18 months, noticed that when the children who had nervous attachment were reunited with their mothers, they were puzzled, dazzled or irritated. However, these kids usually clung to the mother. They remained strong in their mother's attention but seemed unhappy or relaxed. These children's narrow focus and restricted responses discouraged further play and exploration.

WHAT CAUSES ANXIOUS ATTACHMENT?

Researchers aren't completely aware of what causes an individual to form a certain type of attachment through parenting style and behavior.

When people develop an anxious form of attachment, inconsistent parenting may contribute.

A parent with inconsistent parental attitudes may at times be caring and balanced, at times dismissive, emotionally inaccessible or (cold or critical) antipathic.

Parents may also be sluggish or inconsistent in their child's reaction to signs of distress. For example, failure to select a crying baby to prevent the infant from "spoiling" can potentially contribute to a concern for the caregiver.

Failure by a parent or caregiver can leave a child frustrated and unsure because they don't know what conduct to expect.

A child who is nervous about a caregiver will act "clingy" or "luminous" towards them in order to meet their needs.

In nervous attachment, genetics may also play a part.

ANXIOUS ATTACHMENT TRIGGERS.

Due to its general vulnerability, there are many accidents that can trigger someone with anxious attachment knowingly or inadvertently, including:

1. Unresponsiveness.

"A reason why a person with an anxious connection cannot answer a text or call for a long time is their partner," says Lippman-Barile. If you know why your partner doesn't respond, you might worry about what could have happened or what you might have done to drive your partner away. Anxiety at the beginning of a relationship is normal to all, but the rest of the relationship is characterized by people with the anxiety of attachment.

2. Perceived threat or loss of a relationship.
For many, certain conflict levels may be good. But for people with anxiety attachments, communicating authentically about problems can cause fears of loss, says Wegner. If they hear their partners express doubts or concerns about the relationship, they can avoid disaster and immediately conclude that the relationship collapses — sometimes they themselves sabotage.

3. The partner starts acting more independent.
If a partner with a missing relationship wants to make new friends or take on new interests, this may trigger fears of loss and feelings that are not sufficiently interesting. As Lippman-Barile says, the nervous individual may consider joining a book club or taking part alone in a sports game as his SO. Want to leave them.

4. Unpredictable behavior.
"If an anxious person does not know what he/she is to expect from his / her relationship, then this causes a lot of uncertainty for him/her and is very much tied to his / her early attachment towards his / her caregiver.

5. Distance.

People with anxious attachments need constant affirmation, he says, so distance can cause, even if it is perceived. "It could be a partner who goes with friends, who interacts with others, or who is unavailable because of family and work obligations.

SIGNS OF ANXIOUS ATTACHMENT

Children and adults may display signs of anxiety. A child who has formed anxious connections to the caregiver may appear especially worried when separated by the caregiver. They can also be difficult to comfort after the caregiver is done.

In adulthood, a person who develops anxiety can need their partner's constant reassurance and affection. They can also find it difficult to be isolated or alone.

Signs of anxious attachment in children

- Weeping not easily comforted.

- Gets angry when a caregiver leaves.

- Loyalty to their figures.

- Less than children of a similar age exploration.

- Generally tense look.

- Do not associate with foreigners.

- Having trouble managing negative feelings and controlling them.

- Demonstrates violent attitudes and negative relationships between peers.

Signs of anxious attachment in adults

As an adult, anxious attachment style can show up as:

- Hard to believe others

- Poor self-esteem

- fears that the friends will give up

- Closeness and familiarity of desire

- too secure in relationships

- daily reassurance that people care about you

- becoming too sensitive to the actions and moods of a partner

- Be very nervous, impulsive, unpredictable and moody.

Adults and young adults with anxiety can have an elevated risk of anxiety disorders.

Researchers have found that a history of emotional neglect (antipathy) during adolescence was correlated later in life with anxiety disorders in a 2015 study of 160 adolescents and young adults.

These disorders may include:

- social phobia

- generalized anxiety disorder

- panic attacks

In women, these anxiety disorders are more common than in men. Depression is another potential disorder.

How does an anxious attachment pattern develop in children?

A number of factors may contribute to the formation in parents and children of an anxious attachment pattern. The main factors for a child who develops an Anxious/anxious attachment pattern in relation to its primary caregiver are inconsistent accommodation.

Studies have shown that the consistency of parent ties plays a central role in the transition of certain attachment patterns from one generation to the next. An infant thus imitates the parent's Anxious/anxious attachment strategies. Research has also found that the child-rearing behaviors of parents tend to reflect the particular attachment patterns they formed as children with their parents. Parents who grow up with anxiety are therefore not consistent in how they interact with their children, to whom their children respond by developing their own anxiety patterns of attachment.

Many of these parents and caregivers experience strong feelings for their children because of their poor and inconsistent parenting.They are cruel and intrusive in misunderstanding emotional hunger and true child affection. Robert Firestone explains, in his Compassionate Children's Rearing, how parents confuse their desire to love their child for the true love and concern for the well-being of the child. These parents can be overprotective or attempt to live through their child or concentrate on the appearance and success of their child. They also surpass their children's personal limits by touching them inappropriately and violating their privacy.

How does an anxious attachment manifest in adulthood?

Children with anxiety also grow up to worried attachment patterns. As adults, they are self-critical and dangerous. They seek other people's approval and reassurance, but it never relieves their fears. In their relationships, deep feelings of being denied make them anxious and not optimistic. This makes them stick and feel overly dependent on their partner. These people's lives are inconsistent: their vulnerability makes them turn against themselves and their relationships emotionally distressed.

Adults with worried connections sometimes feel desperate and take on the role of the "pursuer" in a relationship. They often have positive views of other people, in particular their parents and their partner, and have a negative view of themselves in general. You rely heavily on your partner to prove your self-worth. As they are insecure because of the incoherence of their caregivers' availability, they are "rejection sensitive," expect rejection or abandonment, and seek signs of a loss of interest for their spouse.

These people are often motivated to take precautionary strategies to avoid being rejected. However, their pathological dependency, expectations and possessiveness tend to reverse the very alienation they fear and precipitate it. Shaver and Clark (1994) have found in relationship theorists and researchers that "pre-occupied" partners tend to be "perpetually attentive and somewhat agitated," resentful and angry that their partner does not give them the attention and reassurance they feel need. They also feel that it is impossible that the other individual will react to them without a dramatic expression of anxiety and anger. Many people with worried attachments fail to express their anger at a partner because of fear of loss or rejection. If you attempt to suppress your rage, your conduct appears to waver between outbursts of wrath and appeals for forgiveness and help. In certain situations, fears and anxieties may cause more extreme emotional upheavals such as depression.

Are certain children at increased risk?
Some experiences in childhood can increase the risk that someone develops this style of attachment, including:

- Early separation from a caregiver or parent

- Childhood difficulty, like physical or sexual violence

- negligence or violence cases

- caregivers who ridiculed them or got angry in trouble

How are patterns of attachment supported by the critical inner voice?

Adults are influenced by destructive thoughts or critical inner voices about themselves, others, and the world in general to enhance depressive beliefs and expectations associated with attachment patterns. These critical voices have a direct impact on a person's relationship style. People with an impaired adult attachment have "voices" that endorse their confidence in the world as a place full of uncertainty and the potential loss of those they love. Examples of their voice attacks include, "It is clear that they're losing interest in you." "He/she still has the excuse that he/she doesn't want to make love." "He/she doesn't love you as much as you love him/her." No wonder she(she) doesn't like you.

HOW ANXIOUS ATTACHMENT STYLE AFFECTS RELATIONSHIPS

Relationships are about giving and taking a lot. They are a back and forth movement of love and affection in their best possible way. Things go smoothly when we are able to adjust to the desires and needs of another person and are able to adapt to us.

However, as most of us know, this sweet and easy interaction of sound is also full of complications. One individual may want closer relationships, while another person needs space. Many people are more anxious and need reassurance, while the other person feels intruded and wants some space.

The explanations for these patterns are very much linked to our early history of attachment. I always say it's the gift that continues to offer in terms of learning how we think, behave and act in our relationships to learn our attachment patterns.

Anxious-Anxious Attachment

When your child feels protected, securely and regularly soothed by your parent, it can create a stable link to that parent. However, if a parent is available and at times, disruptive and disrespectful to others, then the child is more likely to develop an unstable Anxious pattern of attachment. A child with anxiety can feel like it has to stick to its parent to satisfy its needs. They may be disturbed by separation and feel distressed by the parent when they are reunited.

This pattern of attachment will grow when a child experiences emotional hunger directed by the parent, rather than nurturing affection. If a parent is emotionally hungry, they may concentrate on their own needs or search for the infant. For example, if you need an embrace or if you want to be comforted, you can hug the kid. However, the parents may be disturbed or worried about their own needs if the child wants affection or support from the parent.

Parents who are anxiously attached to their child are frequently misconceived of the needs of the child. If they give the boy, they do so in an invasive manner or more of their own. You may be more concerned about the appearance of a good parent than about how you turn in with your children, that is to say, see your children for who they are and give them what you need at the time.

For instance, one mother defined the development of her daughter of elaborate birthday parties. She would dress and be glamorous and look after herself as she would be a "great mother." However, her daughter would feel nervous, insecure and under pressure to behave as the "great little girl" to make her mother look good. The daughter finally felt exhausted and tired of the party that wasn't even about her.

These parents can be overwhelmed by their own fear and are becoming overweight or ignore their children without realizing that. But as they often "get it right" and react with the child tuned, the child will feel helpless and vulnerable to the parent, feeling that he must fuck or make his feelings known to get what he wants.

A child with anxious relations sometimes feels exhausted rather than nurtured by the love of its parent because it is hollow and impaired. You appear to think about your parent and stick to him out of need and sometimes guilt, like taking care of your dad.

A parent who develops an anxious pattern of attachments will overdo his child in an effort to gain "support" and trust. The child does not internalize a sense of security with this kind of connection to the parent. You are left in a state of doubt as to whether you should rely on others. The occasional periods their parent is attuned to cannot benefit because there are so many unpleasant experiences between them.

A parent who has insecure ties to a child also feels this kind of connection as a child. They had their own emotional needs which were not always fulfilled, which left them empty. When you become a mom, you sometimes turn to your child to try to fill your emotional void. This form of attachment is an illustration for the child of how relationships work, and it takes this paradigm into its own adult relationships. And a generational loop of nervous attachment persists.

Anxious-Preoccupied Attachment

If a person is anxiously Anxious as a child with his parent, he or she may become anxiously attached to his partners in a romantic adult relationship. Since they are used to finding someone available incoherently, they appear to feel more vulnerable and seek reassurance in their relationship. At the same time, they may find it hard to trust the terms, warmth and love of their family, because when these words are used by their parents, they are often hollow, missing the true tuned treatment they need.

As adults, you may feel obliged to demand signals that you are valuable to your partner in an effort to ease your anxiety. You may experience emotional hunger for your partner, which is similar to those guided to you by a parent. You can hope that your partner can "rescue" or "complete," a task that any other person cannot carry out. Even as they assume that they are searching for closeness and comfort by sticking to their partner, their desperate acts are actually driving their partner away.

Due to the deep vulnerability from their history, concerned people can be desperate, anxious, demanding, possessive, jealous or dominated to their partner. Sometimes, they falsely perceive the actions of their partners to be rejection or insulting, sometimes thinking things like, "He doesn't love me anymore." "If he really loved me, he would have ..." See how much I do for him, doesn't he? "I wasn't right to trust them." In addition to worrying about or probably because of the feelings of their partners, a person with anxiety may appear to overdo their partner much like their parents overdriven them in an effort to "make them love them."

Although it seems that a person in anxiety is searching for someone who is caring and accessible, they also end up being attracted to a person with an evasive attachment style who fails to fulfil their emotional needs. While this sounds paradoxical, their intense emotions replace the person's missing, genuinely suppressed emotions.

They improve the adaptations of each other in the exhausting dance of their experiences. The avoidant emphasizes his sense of emotional detachment because his partner is so demanding. The concerned partner, in turn, confirms the need to seek and harass the partner as its partner is so remote and secure.

While it is difficult to feel this vulnerability once again, people are always forced to recreate their childhood's emotional environment. That is why it is so important for us to understand and make sense of our attachment types so that we can then improve our relationship with others.

A concerned attachment style can make romantic relationships difficult, but a stable attachment style can be established as an adult.

In order to create more inner stability, we have to consider our own history of connection and our relationship models. With this awareness, we can build a cohesive narrative of our early encounters that gives us an insight into our current relationships.

It can also help to establish relationships with people who are more stable than ours. When we hang in there, even when things get awkward and uncertain, we can adapt to a new kind of relationship and develop a secure attachment.

THE NEGATIVE EFFECTS OF ANXIOUS ATTACHMENT ON INTIMATE RELATIONSHIPS AND HOW TO OVERCOME THEM

The wonder, concern and curiosity so much of a young person has been the subject of pop songs and poetry for many years: What do they do right now? Who are they with? Who are they with? Do they think of me? Do they think of me? However, once a bond has been formed, and two lives have melded, such worries are typically replaced by a relaxed and nuanced awareness of one's partner and, yes, even some form of predictability and routine. However, if these thoughts aren't mitigated by a strong, healthy view of one's own life, they can start to take over, unleashing for both partners a powerful and destructive emotional force that can have catastrophic consequences.

Of course, people are looking for physical closeness to their intimate partners. They want their comfort or help; they can depend on them, and separation is distressing them. The defining characteristics of an individual's attachment to its caregivers during childhood will affect their intimate relationships

Attachment Styles Associated With Anxiety Disorders

A recent study considered parental antipathy or emotional neglect as the antecedent of anxiety disorders. Fear of denial and/or separation as the mediating factor included nervous and Anxious internal working methods. Maternal antipathy included maternal animosity, reluctance, coldness and a scapegoat for your brothers and sisters.

The findings of the study showed the 12-month prevalence of anxiety disorders among adolescents and young adults with ambiguous relationship styles4. The attachment is mildly nervous, with anxiety-Anxious attachment displaying, in particular, the strongest association5 based on a meta-analysis of 46 studies performed with kids between 1984 and 20105.

Anxiety attachment in adults is also closely linked to signs of depression and GAD (generalized anxiety disorder), including fearful-avoidant and worried types. The relation between GAD and anxious attachment most frequently occurs as the scary, avoiding and worrying forms of attachment. Both include hyper-invigilation against perceived threats such as dropping; worry-related cognitions with an emphasis on interpersonal and social areas; and persistent finding attention and treatment of others while such threats occur. A typically pessimistic view of the ability to cope with depression often leads to increased anxiety and is alert about possible threats.

Anxiously Attached Adult and Romantic Relationships
When looking at the impact of adult attachment on romantic relationships, healthy adults are considered to have optimistic perceptions of interpersonal relations and are not afraid of proximity. In comparison, avoiding adults may get anxious if anyone comes near, claims freedom and does not need anyone. Sick adults are clinging types and often have jealousy; they are often afraid that their partner will refuse, so they try to get approval.

Fear of infidelity may become a primary concern for people who are anxiously attached. In a recent study, nervous participants found themselves more willing to receive rejection signals from their partners and were more likely to interpret certain behaviors — sexual, romantic and causative interactions — as fake.

Fears of infidelity and dissolution can also affect adult behavior, which seeks to minimize the risk of infidelity and the breakdown of the relationship. Research in 2016 showed that women and men with higher ratings of nervous romantic attachment exhibit better mate retention behavior.

Behaviors to Keep Your Partner in Relationship

Men tend to display such behaviors more often and usually scored higher in romantic anxiety tests compared with women10. In an evolutionary context, a higher level of mate retention behavior, as cuckoldry and ambiguous paternity spectra was an issue for men11. Men have registered higher scores on behaviors such as direct control, alertness, monopolization, envy, a partner's threat of denial, exploitation of emotional responses and commitments, disrespectful acts, aggression against rival, obedience and degradation and public signals of ownership. Conversely, women tend to use a particular set of retention strategies — in other words, to maximize their beauty, affection, and care.

Anxious Attachment in Intimate Relationships

Although much of this debate focuses on the facets of anxiety about oneself, a relationship impacted by this problem can hardly be uncovered. Many people who are anxiously attached may seem clinging, controlled or even violent. Their anxieties reflect their over-reliance on their partner for support and security – to define and serve their life.

This paradoxically stresses relationships and contributes to lower satisfaction in relationships.

And while this attachment style is a damaging way through the arrangement of one's most intimate relations, it does nothing to reduce the situation by dissolving those relationships. Concerned people will respond to break-ups with angry protests, an all-consuming desire for a former partner, and growing sexual urge to get back and sometimes self-medicate with alcohol or drugs.

HOW CAN A PERSON TRANSFORM AN ANXIOUS ATTACHMENT INTO A SECURE ONE?

Fortunately, the style of attachment of an individual may be updated by means of new experiences and the relationship with a partner with a stable background of communication and psychotherapy. Another successful way of establishing a stable adult relationship is by knowing one's background. Dr Dan Siegel says that "the best predictor of child protection is not what occurred in his parents as children, but rather how his parents feel about the experiences of children." The secret to the "sensibility" of life experiences is to compose a cohesive story that makes them understand how their childhood experiences appear to be a thing of the past.

How to fix an anxious attachment style:
1. Be mindful of your type of attachment.

"Knowledge of attachment styles helps to explain our hidden blocks of confidence, close ties and adult intimacy," says Campbell. Understanding why you appear in relationships is the first step in breaking these patterns. "Each change begins with self-reflection and self-consciousness.

2. Change your actions.

You will start making more informed decisions after being aware of how this connection leads to issues in your relationship. The fear that you normally practice does not contribute to what you really want, says Lippman-Barile. You may make improvements that would result in a stable partnership by choosing otherwise — even though it is terrifying or uncomfortable.

3. Take someone you trust.

Overcoming an anxious type of attachment typically requires support. Getting to your family and friends can be a beginning. Because it is difficult for people with an insecure attachment to trust people close to them, Wegner advises searching for help as well. "It is very normal to have an insecure attachment style and something most therapists can help with," she said. "You can save a lot of hassle down the road by doing some work now."

Because attachment styles are formed to respond to our childish perception of connection, these instinctual patterns can be difficult to overcome. Yet attachment wounds will certainly be healed. These negative habits can be changed with self-awareness and practice.

DO YOU OR YOUR PARTNER HAVE AN ANXIOUS ATTACHMENT?

Relationships are about giving and taking a lot. They are a back and forth movement of love and affection in their best possible way. Things go smoothly when we are able to adjust to the desires and needs of another person and are able to adapt to us. But, as most of us know, this sweet and simple-sounding interaction is often fraught with complications. One individual may want closer relationships, while another person needs space. Many people are more anxious and need reassurance, while the other person feels intruded and wants some space.

The explanations for these patterns are very much linked to our early history of attachment. I often say that knowing our attachment patterns can be a gift to understand how we think, feel, and act in our relationships. In this segment, I'll talk about how an anxious attachment pattern is developed in childhood and how it goes on to affect us in our adult relationships.

AnxiousAttachment

When your child feels protected, securely and regularly soothed by your parent, it can create a stable link to that parent. However, if a parent is available and at times, disruptive and disrespectful to others, then the child is more likely to develop an unstable Anxious pattern of attachment. A child with anxiety can feel like it has to stick to its parent to satisfy its needs. They may be disturbed by separation and feel distressed by the parent when they are reunited.

This pattern of attachment will grow when a child experiences emotional hunger directed by the parent, rather than nurturing affection. If a parent is emotionally hungry, they may concentrate on their own needs or search for the infant. For example, if you need an embrace or if you want to be comforted, you can hug the kid. However, the parents may be disturbed or worried about their own needs if the child wants affection or support from the parent.

Parents who are anxiously attached to their child are frequently misconceived of the needs of the child. If they give the boy, they do so in an invasive manner or more of their own. You may be more concerned about the appearance of a good parent than about how you turn in with your children, that is to say, see your children for who they are and give them what you need at the time. For instance, one mother defined the development of her daughter of elaborate birthday parties. She would dress and be glamorous and look after herself as she would be a "great mother." However, her daughter would feel nervous, insecure and under pressure to behave as the "great little girl" to make her mother look good. The daughter finally felt exhausted and tired of the party that wasn't even about her.

These parents may be overwhelmed by their own fear and uncertainty. They can either overbear or ignore their children without realizing it. But as they often "get it right" and react with the child tuned, the child will feel helpless and vulnerable to the parent, feeling that he must fuck or make his feelings known to get what he wants.

A child with anxious relations sometimes feels exhausted rather than nurtured by the love of its parent because it is hollow and impaired. You appear to think about your parent and stick to him out of need and sometimes guilt, like taking care of your dad.

A parent who develops an anxious pattern of attachments will overdo his child in an effort to gain "support" and trust. The child does not internalize a sense of security with this kind of connection to the parent. You are left in a state of doubt as to whether you should rely on others. The occasional periods their parent is attuned to cannot benefit because there are so many unpleasant experiences between them.

A parent who has insecure ties to a child also feels this kind of connection as a child. They had their own emotional needs which were not always fulfilled, which left them empty. When you become a mom, you sometimes turn to your child to try to fill your emotional void. This form of attachment is an illustration for the child of how relationships work, and it takes this paradigm into its own adult relationships. And a generational loop of nervous attachment persists.

Preoccupied Attachment

If a person is anxiously Anxious as a child with his parent, he or she may become anxiously attached to his partners in a romantic adult relationship. Since they are used to finding someone available incoherently, they appear to feel more vulnerable and seek reassurance in their relationship. At the same time, they may find it hard to trust the terms, warmth and love of their family, and when these terms are used by their parents, they are often hollow, missing the true tuned treatment they need.

As adults, you may feel obligated to demand signals that you are valuable to your partner in an effort to ease your anxiety. You may experience emotional hunger for your partner, which is similar to those guided to you by a parent. You can hope that your partner can "rescue" or "complete," a task that any other person cannot carry out. Even though they assume that they are searching for closeness and comfort by sticking to their partner, their desperate acts are actually driving their partner away.

Due to their past deep-seated vulnerability, people in a relationship can be anxious, insecure, greedy, possessive, jealous and dominated towards their partners. Sometimes, they falsely perceive the actions of their partners to be rejection or insulting, sometimes believing things like, "He doesn't love me anymore." "If he really loved me, he would have ..." See how much I do love him, don't he? "I wasn't right to trust them." In addition to worrying about or probably because of the feelings of their partners, a person with anxiety may appear to overdo their partner much like their parents overdriven them in an effort to "make them love them." Though it seems like a person with anxiety is searching for someone who is caring and accessible, they also end up being attracted to a person with an evasive relationship style who fails to fulfil their emotional needs. Although this sounds paradoxical, their extreme emotions replace the person's missing, genuinely suppressed emotions. They improve the adaptations of each other in the exhausting dance of their experiences. The avoidant emphasizes his sense of relational detachment because his partner is so demanding. The concerned partner, in turn, confirms the need to seek and harass the partner as its partner is so remote and secure. While it is difficult to feel this vulnerability once again, people are always forced to recreate their childhood's emotional environment. Therefore, it is so important to understand and make sense of our attachment patterns so that we can change our relationship style.

A concerned attachment style can make romantic relationships difficult, but a stable attachment style can be established as an adult. This is a subject I will talk about in the online workshop "Developing a secure link." To create more internal security, we must know our own history of attachment and the roots of our relationship models. With this awareness, we can build a cohesive narrative of our early encounters that gives us an insight into our current relationships.

It can also help to establish relationships with people who are more stable than ours. When we hang in there, even when things get awkward and uncertain, we can adjust to a new kind of relationship and develop a stable attachment.

THE AVOIDANT ATTACHMENT STYLE

Human beings are habituated creatures, and through an unconscious impulse to revive and fix the problems of our past, we will attract the same kind of partners and trap ourselves in a destructive loop.

Some may do this because they have an insecure style of attachment, which is how they form bonds and interact with others.

According to psychotherapist Allison Abrams, one form is known as "avoiding attachment." She told Business Insider that our childhood experiences form our attachment style, then the blueprint for how we deal with future relationships.

"Insecure types of attachment, including avoiding attachment, typically stem from some kind of early trauma," she said. "If our primary caregivers do not reliably meet our needs, we have the belief that they will not satisfy any significant other [and] that we can never rely on others."

In essence, it is a defensive mechanism, and people with avoided attachment can avoid relationships completely or keep any new people they meet at a distance. You may sabotage your blooming romances from nowhere because they're afraid that their new partner is going to leave them — so they first get inside.

"This is an implicit attempt to ensure that they never go through anything like the initial caregiver they went through," said Abrams. "The irony is that we have learned to use this security to recreate what we were trying to avoid."

AVOIDANT PEOPLE FIND FAULTS IN ANYONE

Instead of allowing a relationship to evolve naturally, an avoidant prefers to live in places in which he is dissatisfied. Although people with healthy types of attachment may compromise and concentrate on the better, people who resist can't. They focus on small faults and imagine how happy they were or how lucky they could be to meet someone else.

Not only do they injure themselves. And they do not injure themselves. Sometimes they attract people with nervous commitment, who give up their own desires to satisfy their partners. Shockingly unhappy people become anxious to be too much or too little for the person they are dating and take it unbelievably personally.

Often, they play games in their relationship to gain attention in an effort to relieve the anxiety. They can take action, attempt to jealously make their partner or cancel and avoid replying to texts or calls.

Unfortunately, this makes the avoidants an enticing match. Concerned people live out their experience because the fear of abandonment and abuse of an unavailable person feels familiar. The evader of a pair has someone that always watches them, even if they make no effort.

Although the anxiety of the anxious person is justified, the avoiding person is safe in the knowledge that her partner will not harm her. It's a recognized — but toxic — loop.

It is well known that baby relationships have a deep impact on their long-term well-being in the first years of their life.

When babies have access to warm, responsive careers, they will grow up with a strong, secure attachment to the caregivers.

On the other hand, if babies do not have this connection, they may build a bad attachment to these caregivers. This can influence the relationships that they develop during their lives.

A child who is firmly attached to its caregiver has a variety of benefits, including enhanced emotional control and increased trust, and an increased capacity to display love and empathy towards others.

UNDERSTANDING INSECURE AVOIDANT ATTACHMENT

Securely attached children can better control their feelings, feel more positive in their own life and appear to be more compassionate and caring than insecure children.

In comparison, parents who are generally unaware, far or disruptive cause significant distress for their children. Children adapt to this atmosphere of rejection by building protection attachments in an attempt to feel safe, modulate or tone down intense emotional conditions and reduce frustration and pain. They are one of three dysfunctional parent relationship patterns (an avoidant, Anxious/fearful, or disorganized/fearful). In this article, we explain evasive patterns of attachment that have been found to account for around 30% of the general population.

WHAT IS AVOIDANT ATTACHMENT?

In babies and infants, and evacuating relationship is created where parents or caregivers are either not emotionally accessible or unaccountable.

Babies and children must be close to their caregivers. However, they can fast learn to avoid or block their overt emotional displays. If children become conscious that if they show themselves, they will be rejected by the parent or caregiver, then they adapt.

If children with avoiding attachment do not satisfy their inner need for connection and physical contact, they stop searching for closeness or expressing emotion.

Parents of children with an evasive attachment are emotionally inaccessible or sometimes unable to respond. You neglect or disregard the needs of your children and may deny them, especially when your child is injured or ill. These parents often prevent their children from crying and promote premature autonomy.

In response, the evasive attached child learns early in his life to suppress the normal desire to seek comfort from his parent when scared, upset or in pain. Joint researcher Jude Cassidy explains how these children cope: "In many stressful and traumatic experiences with people rejecting attachments, they learned that acknowledging and showing discomfort leads to rejection or punishment. They also can at least partially fulfil one of the needs of attachment by failing to weep or communicate their feelings externally.

Children who have an evasive relationship with a parent appear to withdraw from their body needs. Any of these children are highly dependent on self-alimenting, self-alimenting behavior. They establish a pseudo-independent attitude towards life and sustain the illusion of being able to look after themselves fully. As a consequence, they have no incentive or encouragement to seek assistance or help from other people.

WHAT BEHAVIORS ARE ASSOCIATED WITH AVOIDANT ATTACHMENT IN CHILDREN?

Many precautious, self-contained "little adults" have already become more like infants. As noted, the key protective attachment tactic used by more with evasive attachment is to never outwardly express a desire for closeness, comfort, affection or love. On a physiological level, however, when their heart rates and galvanic skin responses are assessed during experimental separation, their reactions and anxiety are as high as other children. Avoidantly attached children tend to search for closeness, to try to get closer to their connection, while not communicating directly or connected.

In one such experiment, Mary Ainsworth, the "Strange Situation" technique, studied the reactions of 1-year-olds during separation and reunion encounters. When their mother returned to their room, they "prevented or actively avoided contact with their mother." According to Dan Siegel, even very little children "intuitively believe that their parents are not able to know them, which gives them a profound sense of isolation," when the parents are distant or withdrawn.

WHAT CAUSES AVOIDANT ATTACHMENT?

Sometimes, when facing a child's emotional needs, parents may feel exhausted or nervous and close themselves emotionally.

They can completely neglect the emotional needs or communication of their child. You will isolate yourself from the child if you need love or comfort.

These parents may be extremely cruel or insensitive when their child has a time of great need such as scary, sick or hurt.

Parents who encourage a preventative commitment to their children often freely dismay emotional displays, such as weeping when they are unhappy or bleeding when joyful.

Although very young children have unreasonable perceptions of mental and functional freedom.

Some habits that may encourage babies and children to escape attachment include one parent or caregiver, who:

- consistently refuses to accept the cries or other signs of distress or fear of your child

- deliberately inhibit the emotion of your infant, asking it to stop crying, growing up or hardening.

- Gets angry or physically removed from a child by displaying signs of fear or distress.

- Shames an infant for emotional shows

- has unreasonable perceptions of their child's emotional and realistic freedom

SIGNS OF AVOIDANT ATTACHMENT

- To form connections with unlikely possibilities, for example, with a married individual.

- Avoid physical contact – do not want women, go ahead with several measures or don't want the same bed.

- Hold secrets or leave unknown things.

- Mental examination during interactions with a partner.

- Take out when things go well.

- Flirting with others to introduce tension into the relationship.

- The idealization of past relations.

- Complaining that they are dominated, smothered, suffocated and/or too vulnerable.

- Frequently deny other people's attempts to support, aid or share.

HOW DOES AN AVOIDANT ATTACHMENT DEVELOP IN CHILDREN?

Why is it difficult for some parents, who actively want the best for their kids, to stay tuned or be emotionally close to their children? Attachment researchers have found many explanations for the difficulties of parents in this area. Studying a number of emotionally remote mothers, researchers found that mothers lack a response to their children at least partly because they lacked knowledge of "how to help others." Some of these mothers lacked empathy, while others lacked a sense of close relationship and dedication, which seemed crucial to "motivating treatment."

In other words, the mothers treated their infants as well as infants in this study, and now their babies are an avoiding attachment to the baby. Further "evidence for intergenerational transmission of an attachment style" was presented by a recent meta-review of attachment research; it has also shown important links between parents' evading styles of care for children and the avoidance attachment to their child, especially in the case of older children and adolescents.

THE AVOIDANT/DISMISSIVE ATTACHMENT STYLE IN ADULTS

Many who developed an evasive attachment to their parents or parents when they grew up have what is called an adult rejection attachment. Because they have learned as children to separate themselves from their physical needs and diminish the value of feelings, in romantic relationships, they often clear of emotional proximity. Discarded adult persons often seek out relationships and spend time with their partner, but when the relationships are too close, they may become uncomfortable. You may view your partners as "wanting too much" or clinging if your partner shows an emotionally closer desire.

In the face of separation or loss challenges, many cynical men and women will concentrate their attention on other issues and goals. Others prefer to retreat and try themselves to face a threat. They deny their weakness and use repression to control emotions in situations where their attachments are triggered. When seeking support from a spouse in a crisis, indirect strategies such as hinting, lamentation and sulking are likely to be used.

According to Attachment Researchers Fraley and Brumbaugh, many adults who have been rejected use pre-emptive tactics to deactivate the attachment mechanism, for example, may opt not to become involved in a close relationship out of fear of rejection. A second strategy is to remove reminders of unpleasant relationship incidents, such as a breakdown. In fact, adults reported their early relationship with parents as a dismissing study. Others may characterize their childhood as happy when their parents love, but cannot give specific examples to support these positive assessments.

People with this type of attachment tend to be too focused on themselves and their own creature comforts and often ignore other people's feelings and interests. They sometimes find it hard to tell their partner about their thoughts and feelings. Their typical response to the dispute, confrontation and other stressful circumstances is to be remote and distant.

Discontinued adults also have an excessively optimistic view of themselves and a harshly negative outlook towards others. This high self-esteem is protective in many situations and preserves a fragile self, extremely vulnerable to mildew, ridicule and other narcissistic injuries. It typically acts as a cure for low self-esteem and self-hatred feelings. According to Phil Shaver and Mario Mikulincer, adult attachment experts, evasive partners frequently respond angrily to perceive difficulties or other challenges, for example, when the other party fails to endorse or confirm its inflatable identity.

HOW ARE PATTERNS OF ATTACHMENT SUPPORTED BY THE CRITICAL INNER VOICE?

The negative, distrustful and aggressive attitude towards other people which are connected to a dismissive style of attachment is exacerbated by harmful thoughts or critical inner voices. The excessively optimistic and often benign views of oneself, which many avoiding individuals encounter, are often encouraged by the inner voice, frequently covering up vicious and self-degrading thoughts. Both kinds of voices towards oneself and others are part of an internal model, based on the earliest attachments of an individual, which serve as a guide to how to communicate with a romantic partner. The vital inner voice can be regarded as the language of these internal models; the voice serves as a negative filter through which the people look at themselves, their partners and relations.

While many vital inner voices are only partially aware, they do have the power to influence how people in near, most intimate relationships respond to each other. Individuals with a dismissing attachment style have indicated that they have certain thoughts:

- "You need anybody."

- "Don't be concerned too much. You're just going to be disappointed.

- "Men will not participate in a partnership."

- "Women's going to try to pick you up."

- "Why does he/she question you so much?

- "You have to put up a lot to stay in a man/woman."

85

- "Some things in life are more important than romance."

- "You must defend yourself.

- In this relationship, you will be harmed.

- "For him/her, you're too sweet."

Avoidant Attachment Style in Relationships

We all know that one person can't deal with proximity. Maybe it's the man who works for 80 hours on the weekend wants his "me time," but he can't plan more than one night a week. Or it is the woman who, after a casual date, fills her social calendar but never takes something seriously. These people have what is called an "avoiding type of attachment."

"Avoiders also implicitly claim that they are not available when the subject transforms into spring with friends or a romantic partner," life coach Chuck Rockey says. "They often choose things wrong with a partner to concentrate on them as excuses for distancing themselves from their colleagues and then lament the lack of interaction. Of course, they often do it on their own, and it takes a while for them to realize that it is an unsatisfactory state of affairs."

According to psychologists, this way of dealing with others actually relies on how the "avoiders" perceived childhood intimacy. And while it comes from years and years of being in the grasp of others, even the most committed evacuees will learn to feel secure with the intimacy they seek from their partners.

Identifying an avoidant attachment style

There are two kinds of evasive attachment styles: rejector-evident, frightening or anxious-evitative, explains Seaside Therapy Center owner and therapist Rachel (Bauder) Cohen, MSW, LCSW. Someone who has a rejecting-avoiding relationship style frequently sees himself as alone and "go it alone."

"A person with a fearful-evitating attachment-style performs a balancing act," explains Cohen. These people fear that they will lose themselves so that they will send out mixed signals: drive their partner away and withdraw them later. They still have few close friendships, since they fear losing and finishing alone.

How to tell if someone is avoidant

Although it is never a good idea to diagnose your spouse or yourself, certain behaviors or patterns may be seen by an evident individual. The Double Trust Dating specialist David Bennett reports that a variety of signs are to be found:

- Maintaining a shallow relationship or surface level

- Focus on physical contact without emotional proximity

- Race "hot and cold" with your love

- Delete when someone begins to close

- Risk tolerance

- Abuse of relationships repeatedly

"If you are afraid of privacy, feel trapped in it, frustrated, always think of breaking up with your partner, or regret that you broke up with your partner some time ago, you probably have a style of avoidance.

"If you dig deeper into the features of the various attachment styles, you generally know where you are.

What causes an avoidant attachment style

People with avoiding attachment "come through it frankly" and learn their attachment style very early from their parents. Parents of children who are ignored are for much of the time emotionally unavailable or unaccompanied, which teach children not to rely on their love. Studies show that these parents ignore or disregard the needs of their children, prevent crying and contribute to an exceptionally active early childhood.

Since they have not been rewarded for sharing emotions as children, it is also difficult for eviting adults to cope with that kind of intimacy as they age. Notice that discovering these roots is a good starting point to decide if you or your partner are preventative. "This will allow you to more critically see the trends as a response to your experience as young children. This is the first step towards safer, healthier attachment.

Do You or Your Partner Have an Avoidant Attachment Pattern?

I asked a random group of people if they felt they were the prosecutor or the distanced guy. In other words, did you see yourself as the one who usually wants to see closeness and affection or who usually needs time and space more alone? Almost everyone we talked had an immediate response both to yourself and to your partner.

Most of us are aware of our relationship pattern. We may feel ready to go "all in" in the matter of love or maybe afraid of being "locked" down. However, we do not know how far these behaviors relate back to our earliest relationships and the patterns of attachment which we developed towards our caretakers.

Knowing our attachment patterns can be a gift that continues to deliver in terms of understanding how we are thinking, feeling and behaving in our ties. In this section, I'm concentrating on evasive childhood attachment, which sometimes becomes a dismissive and avoidable attachment in adulthood. This attachment pattern arises when a child is not regularly healthy, heard, or reassured by the parent and becomes pseudo-independent.

A child with an avoidant attachment seeks to fulfil its own needs since it is too difficult to react to others. They build a sense of embarrassment, thinking, "Not worth paying attention to." They then withdraw from their needs to escape this embarrassment.

As adults, the same pseudonym can lead the person to be self-contained and disdainful when he communicates his needs or a desire for emotional closeness. About 30 percent of people have a preventative attachment trend according to attachment study. Let's then take a closer look at what that entails.

Avoidant Attachment in Children

To build a healthy bond, a child must feel secure, seen and reassured by the caregiver. Parental behaviors that lead to the development of a parental-child relationship include the parent's removal, exclusion, emotional removal, or unawareness of the emotional needs of the child while addressing fundamental needs of the child, such as food and shelter. This kind of parent can be described as an "emotional desert," since they are not very sensitive. For instance, the parent cannot even hear the baby when he starts crying or learning the signs of his baby. They will also be upset or depressed. They may be distant from their own interests and not attentive to the needs of their children as an extension.

The baby experiences a sort of emotional neglect in this case. My daddy, psychologist Robert Firestone, has called them "love food," a kind of tuned emotional nutrition and parental warmth, particularly in the first year. In their absence, the child may realize that behaving as they do is the best way to deal with their anger about not meeting their needs. As Dr Daniel Siegel puts it, the child learns to withdraw, because they are frustrated that their parents are not happy with them. They internalize the idea that it's "dust."

In the now-famous experiment "The Odd Situation," created by attachment researcher Mary Ainsworth, a pattern of attachment of a child and parent is assessed based on their reunion behavior. In the experiment, the child plays with his parent in a bed. A stranger (researcher) enters and leaves his parent. The parent then returns, comforts the child and leaves the researcher again. The researcher then returns, and the parent follows.

If the parent leaves, a tightly attached child may feel distressed, but go to the parent for comfort until he returns. Then they feel soothed and can come back to play. There is no obvious reaction to the parent leaving the room with an avoiding infant. A heart monitor on the child; however, shows that the entire time the parent leaves the room, his heart rate returns to normal until the parent returns. In other words, you are worried about separation, but you adapted and learned not to show it to prevent your parents from being shamed of the expected lack of response.

An avoiding child adapts to his or her situations by being pseudo-independent, seeking ways to mask or meet their needs. They may appear to be more independent or inward. Furthermore, it is much easier for a child to pretend that something is wrong than acknowledging the grim truth that something is wrong with their parents. If the child viewed its parent as being absent, it would lose a sense of protection that is necessary for their survival. It can also alter life to overcome experiences of attachment in adulthood. As an adult who is not reliant anymore on survival caregiver, a person can face the pain of having imperfect parents comfortably and stop integrating the deficits in his parent's identity.

Dismissive-Avoidant Attachment in Adults

A person who has grown up under an evasive pattern of attachment is more likely to develop a dismissive pattern of attachment in relation to their partners and/or children. In a romantic relationship, a person with an evasive attachment pattern may be more aloof or reject, as the name implies. They want to be in a relationship, but at the same time, they do not want or need emotional closeness. You may appear to seek solitude, distancing yourself emotionally from your partner. You may tend to concentrate more on yourself and to place your interests over your partner's. They can appear calm and detached and sometimes display frustration or resentment when their partner communicates their feelings or needs, or when their partner thinks they are "childish" or "dramatic."

It is also difficult for a person to recognize himself as having a pattern of avoidable attachment because just as they see the desires and needs of their spouse as "too much" or overwhelming, they see their own desires and needs as well. Thus, they may see themselves as indicators of an insecure attachment pattern, as "needy" simply because they want others. If the value of a loved one may be denied or if you are faced with danger from leaving, your attachment mechanism will be triggered, and you may feel very distressed at the possibility of real loss. It may also make it much harder for them to realize that they are avoidable.

HOW CAN WE TRANSFORM A DISMISSING/AVOIDANT ATTACHMENT INTO A SECURE ONE?

Fortunately, we don't have to stay stuck within the boundaries of the defensive attachment mechanisms we built early in life.

There are many encounters in life that provide opportunities for personal development and transformation. Although your patterns of attachment were established in infancy and continue throughout your life, it is possible to establish an "Earned Stable Attachment"at any age.

Attachment research shows that if we cannot make sense of and experience the full pain of our experiences, we are much more likely to replicate it. We are inclined to form the same attachment pattern with our own children that we encountered ourselves, hence, perpetuating the pattern for generations. However, by constructing a cohesive narrative of our story and allowing ourselves to feel the pain of how we were harmed, we can break damaging relationship habits and create more stable attachments. We should understand why we're struggling in our relationships and consciously question habits that were prescribed to us by our experience.

If we identify with having a negative attachment pattern, we should strive to have compassion for ourselves. After all, we made this adaptation for our psychological survival. We should start to question a "critical inner voice" that might tell us we are "worthless and unimportant" or that our thoughts and desires are "too much.

Can you prevent avoidant attachment?
In order to ensure that you and your child build a healthy relationship, it is important to know how you fulfil their needs. Be aware of the messages that you send to them about their feelings. You can start by ensuring you are happy with warmth and affection with all their basic needs, such as shelter, food and proximity.

When you rock them to sleep, sing to them. Speak to them warmly as you change the diaper.

When they scream, pick them up to soothe them. Don't shame them, like spills or broken dishes, because of common fears or mistakes.

THE BEST RELATIONSHIPS FOR AN AVOIDANT ATTACHMENT STYLE.

Looking at the definitions of all three styles, it's easy to look at the obvious folks and think they're "the bad ones." But this isn't true — there's no "evil" style of connecting with other people. You're looking for what you're looking for. The needs, interests and expectations of none are less true than those of someone else.

If your attachment form is preventative, you can also use this information to help select a compatible partner since certain attachment styles would certainly benefit you better than others.

Another evasive person, for instance, is not your best option, since they will appear to walk away when relationship issues occur, as they inevitably do. A happy couple always needs at least one partner who is able to stick through the good times to get through the bad patches.

A nervous person isn't a good idea for you either. In fact, the combination of anxious and evasive is the worst combination of attachment types because you have opposite intimacy needs: anxious ones want proximity while evaders value autonomy. As a result of the nervous individual, being driven away, becomes much more optimistic and encouraging, a desire that only drives the avoiding partner further away. It's probably a terrible situation you want to stop.

This leaves people with stable attachments — and for romantic partners, they should be your top pick. Safe people are usually better able to understand and tolerate your evasive nature and change their relationship standards to take your privacy, freedom and alone time into account. Fortunately, you are also the main demographic group for intimate partners – those with stable attachments.

Healing avoidant attachment.

You can also change your behavior. If your attachment style does not reflect how you want to be in your relationships individually, there are ways of changing your answers. Self-consciousness is the first step towards changing yourself.

"The human brain can be fickle but is unbelievably complex, evolving and can build healthy new habits and ways of love," writes Linda Carroll, M.S. at mbg, marriage counsellor. "Practice of consciousness is vital for any transition. Relationships will lift us from our early attachment habits into a healthier, safer and better style."

If you want to be closer to a partner than you normally would like to be, try your instinctive desire for independence in a different way: by realizing that you can choose to be more intimate independently, it is your choice to do so and not to force something upon you. The couple can also be limited: maybe close at weekends but keep a lot of time alone during the week, or vice versa. The point is, you can switch to more intimacy in phases, when you feel comfortable, without losing all your privacy.

FEARFUL/ANXIOUS-AVOIDANT ATTACHMENT STYLE

Imagine feeling lonely inside and longing for love and affection. Then you meet someone awesome. You are filled with joy and enthusiasm. You should feel all right now as you know you ought to.

But a few months later, when your romantic partner wraps his arms around you and tells you that you love them, you feel a surge of fear and inevitable doom. You're trying to be happy, and you know what an "average" person would feel like. But it is difficult for you to conceal your fear. You attempt to correct it by describing it, but this effort just keeps you calm and required. Over the next few weeks, you can experience squabbles, begin to take signs of a second thought from your wife and get this horrible feeling in your stomach ... you know the one that you spend your life trying to stop. When the relationship starts to muddle, you just want to cry, "What happened?"

What happened is that you ran directly into your own protective wall, the part of your personality the wants to defend you and defend you. Naturally, this response is not a logical process; it resides in the emotional centers of the brain and is activated automatically by environmental signals. You don't care for your logical reasoning or the desire for love and affection for adults. You'd rather be miserable and alone rather than hurt.

The theory of attachment can give us a deeper understanding of this process. In infancy, the attachment system raises anxiety when the young person remains too far from his parent; the resulting malaise then drives the child to regain proximity. Imagine what happens if the parent you are looking for is scared or ashamed of himself. If the parent screams at the coming child or worse become physically violent, the "attachment figure" is as bad as something from which the child escaped first.

A frightened parent (who may be a victim of violence himself) can also not sufficiently console a distraught infant. The attachment device does not fulfil its intended purpose in either situation. The child cannot recover from the environment distress and cannot be relieved by the parent. In order to make things worse, the actions of the parent may increase the fear of the child and prevent the child from approaching the scary parent again.

Children raised in these environments are hyper-vigilant for risks (such as those with anxious/careful attachments) while simultaneously avoiding emotional closeness and intimacy (such as those with evasive / disappearing attachments). When seen in lab conditions ("strange circumstance" model of Mary Ainsworth), these children can be seen approaching the parent only for freezing, withdrawing or walking purposefully. In the same way, as adults, at the same time they want closeness and affection and approach possible attachment figures (close friends or romantic partners), but then get extremely uncomfortable when they get close to and withdraw with the partners so that the message given to others "come here and go." This person cannot know that he is indeed the one who separates and rejects it.

If in these explanations and trends, you see yourself, take heart. The protective mechanism is a natural response to childhood stress. The stressor may have been physical violence or aggression (big 't' trauma) or frustrated animosity and traumatic parenthood (little 't' trauma). Parental worries don't necessarily mean the parent was directly threatening. A parent who is deprived or mentally ill can be scary, so the child knows that the parent cannot protect or console them.

Dr Ed Tronic's work with young children with the "Still Face Model" offers a clear example of the consequences of parental distraction. If parents fail to portray and evaluate the emotional experiences of their children adequately, the children become emotionally dysregulated. If continued for a longer period of time, this trend may have a lasting effect on the neurology of the developing child and his ability to interpret and correctly control emotions and to maintain safe and mutually reciprocal ties.

WHAT IS FEARFUL-AVOIDANT ATTACHMENT?

Fearful and avoidable attachment is a type of attachment (as it is in relationships) that is both nervous and avoiding. It is often referred to the as disorganized attachment. In a study published in the Journal of Sex & Marital Therapy in 2019, the frightening-avoiding attachment is described as "reticent to engaging in close connections and the need to be loved by others."

A fast introduction to all attachment styles: people who grow up with trustworthy parents who worked faithfully with them (including a lot of love and care) typically have a sure attachment and have stable relationships where they feel secure, valued and willing to love. They usually have strong relationships. Many with unstable or non-existent parental relationships appear to end up with fragile attachment that can fall into two categories: nervous attachment or preventative attachment. People with an anxious style are fond of attachment and sometimes become "needy," while those with an avoiding style of attachment prefer to do the reverse, driving them away from a fear of intimacy.

However, fear-evitating type of attachment requires a mixture of both anxiety and love. Psychologists Nicolas Favez and Herve Tissot say that the researchers behind the 2019 study seldom speak about the type of attachment and are not well known since that type is much rarer than the other three types of attachment. Some research has found that "the most psychological and emotional threats" are formidable and avoiders.

The frighteningly evasive attachment style is characterized by a negative perception of oneself and another. Those that fall into this category consider themselves as undignified and incapable of devotion. In addition, they believe like others are unworthy of their love and respect because they expect others to reject or harm them. Owing to their negative self-interest and the belief that others are likely to injure them, those who have a fearfully avoided relationship style prefer to avoid near contact with others to protect themselves against expected rejection.

In certain ways, this scary style of attachment resembles that which refuses attachment, since it both contributes to a person rejecting attachments. However, frighteningly attached persons have negative self-respect and thus rely on others to retain a positive outlook on themselves. This need for acceptance also makes them dependent on their partner, even if they are very reluctant to join. Having said this, fearful avoiding partners are less likely to be attached and show affection than concerned partners, since they expect that when they attempt, they will be rejected.

The frightening-eviting attachment style can be one of the hardest to recognize. It is characterized by a strong desire to protect oneself and escape relationships while also strongly wanting to be in a relationship. On the other hand, the most common models of a fearful-avoidant style involve a willingness to be in relationship with someone, but at the same time to feel insecure confronting someone, persistent anxiety that one will suffer if someone makes a negative perception of oneself and overall.

Due to the self-awareness encountered by a fear-avoidant person, they become dependent and may fight against separation. It is difficult for them to establish trust and therefore avoid confrontation. They lack emotion and are vulnerable to their partners unless they are confident that they will receive a positive response. Many who are afraid of entering a relationship appear to be nervous and have spent more in the relationship than their partners. They prefer to internalize relationship issues as their liability and play a passive role in the relationship. Owing to all the doubts and worries that someone has come to know and continues with a relationship, fearfully attached individuals frequently tend to avoid interpersonal encounters with others physically and emotionally.

It can be difficult to grasp this type of attachment. There's a list of the most common symptoms characterizing the fearful-avoiding attachment style if you are still uncertain where you are:

- A poor self-confidence

- Negative opinion of others

- The ability to be linked to others with great reluctance

- Fear of denial

- Fear of renunciation

- A feeling that you are not good enough or deserving

- Worries that you want to leave or quit partnerships

- Hard to believe others

- Feel more confident than most in your relationships

- Take a very long time for a relationship, but seem to be dependent when it starts

- Aim to stop confrontation excessively

- How much you talk about yourself and your emotions is hesitant and reserved

- In partnerships tend to be passive

- It is very difficult to break off ties because of the fear of not having another partner.

- Severe problems controlling the emotions

- a poor or inadequate reaction to negative emotions

- The negative view of yourself

- to view and help other people negatively

- Less romantic relationship engagement and satisfaction

- Higher chance of conflict in relationships

- A very large number of sexual partners

- More sexual conformity (You probably say yes when you ask for sex)

- High anxiety

- Fear of intimate relationships or fear of partnerships

"Fearful avoidance or depression has also been shown to be associated with restricted disorders of personality or dissociative symptoms.

If you read this, and I think I describe your attachment behavior, I'm excited about you because you have the power and awareness to start forming your attachment behavior. I think, once you understand your attachment style, and the way you deal with your romantic partner, that you have the ability to change some of these patterns.

WHAT CAUSES FEARFUL-AVOIDANT ATTACHMENT?

Some studies suggest that trauma could be a key factor in creating terrifying and avoiding attachment.

As children, they respond to stress with "apparently incoherent conducts" through fearful avoidance, they describe how they are aimless, afraid of their caregivers or hostile towards their caregivers. Previous studies have speculated that such behavior is the product of traumatic contact with the caregiver such that the child "constantly fetches between deactivation and hyperactivation (the presence of the 'fearing' figure constantly activates attachment needs). "

In other words, a child who is afraid of its caregiver desperately needs comfort but knows that the person giving it cannot trust it. In adulthood, you both feel like you want intimacy but instinctively fear it and try to escape it.

HOW FEARFUL-AVOIDANT ATTACHMENT AFFECTS RELATIONSHIPS.

The report, which analyzed 600 men and women on their relationships and sexual lives, discovered that people with terrifying and evasive commitment appear to have much more sexual partners than others. Fearful evaders have appeared to be a lot more sexually compliant, so when someone asks for sex, you will most probably say yes — so that when asked for, you have sex even if you do not have any sexual desire.

It can be fun to have a lot of sex. When you are alone, it often means exploring, meeting new people and having new experiences, many of which are deliciously low pressure, at present. But, while some people are aware of many casual sexual experiences for physical pleasure, excitement and other purposes, it seems that terrifying and avoiding people may have a great deal of sex with many different people without a lot of justification at all.

Why? Favez and Tissot theorized that it was linked to the "out-of-control behavior" formed as a reaction to the uncertainty between both desiring ties and feel repelled by it. They explain: they explain:

"For example, sexual interaction can be initiated in order to meet the emotional needs of depression or to escape from thoughts that lead to depression," they write. "The high anxiousness felt in fearful evasion can encourage the individual to become closer to a partner through sexual activity, while the high evasive propensity can almost simultaneously motivate the individual to break the link with the partner ... which is followed by a search for a new partner.

Now it's not terrible to have a lot of sex by itself. But to do this out of a combined desire and fear of touch, even when you don't really want sex yourself? That might quickly be exhausting and perhaps even damaging, particularly if you start saying yes to sex, or sex that jeopardizes your physical well-being. If you also sever connections with people if you really want to come closer to them, you have a lot of heart and mind due to your own fears.

HOW THE ANXIOUS-AVOIDANT COUPLE CAN FIND GREATER SECURITY

Individuals with a fearful evading attachment style want close ties, but feel insecure dependent on others and fear that they will be discarded. One of the four main attachment types suggested by psychologist John Bowlby, who has developed attachment theory, is fearful avoidants.

Annexation theory is a theory in psychology which explains how and why we have close ties with others.

According to attachment theory, our early life experiences can lead us to establish perceptions that influence our life-long relationships.

Persons with a frightening avoidable attachment style are worried that they are rejected and unhappy with their close relationships.

The frightening evasive style of attachment is connected with negative results such as the increased risk of social anxiety and depression and less satisfying interpersonal relations.

Recent research suggests that the attachment style can be modified and better approaches can be created to communicate with others.

THE CHALLENGES OF ANXIOUS-AVOIDANT RELATIONSHIPS

There are so many different ways to be unhappy with love, but the modern psychology focuses on relationships, very various in which one party has been described as eviting in its attachment patterns, and the other as anxious. Attachment Theory is a concept given to a whole series of theories about how we love and how the English psychologist John Bowlby created it in the '50s and '60s. It divides humanity into three groups according to our various abilities to conduct relationships of confidence and honesty.

Second, people are firmly attached and who have stable and pleasant childhood memories, and now expect to be treated kindly by those they love, the lucky kind who are empathetic and compassionate – who interact frankly who straightforwardly with their needs. Around 50 % of the population is thought to be securely connected. This leaves two interesting health differences caused by some kind of early parental dislocation and trauma: the first type is called Avoidant, while the second is considered to be Anxious. What makes it even more difficult and fuel-efficient is that levitators and disquieters are always attracted to pairs (this is part of their pathology) where their complex emotional peculiarities lead to a very volatile mix. An anxiously attached person in a connection would feel that he is not valued and respected properly. They would – they say – like so much closer ties, tenderness, touch and sex, and they are persuaded that such a union can be possible. Yet they seem to be humiliatingly and hurtfully separated from the person they are with. They never seem to want them as much as they can. Their coldness and isolation profoundly mourn them and eventually they slip into moods of self-loathing and rejection, feeling unrecognized and confused and revengeful and rancorous. They could remain silent for a long time about their grievances before desperation finally erupts. While it's a very inappropriate moment (perhaps they are tired and their partner is over midnight), they won't be able to concentrate on dealing with these issues right now. Predictably, those fights are going very poorly. The nervous lover loses his calmness, exaggerates and pushes his points so violently that his wife is persuaded that he is insane and cruel.

A stable spouse may be able to ease the situation, but an avoidant definitely doesn't. This evasive party causes all the fear known to its nervous lover. The avoiding partner unconsciously withdraws under pressure to be warmer and closer together and feels frustrated and struck. They go cold – and withdraw from the situation further raises the discomfort of the partner. Under their silence, the avoidant resents a sense of being 'ordered,' as they put it: they have the feeling of being wrongly oppressed and irritated by the 'neediness' of the other. They could secretly imagine sex with someone else, preferably a total stranger, or going to the other room and reading a book, but probably not one about psychology. It helps you tremendously to realize that this is not just your relationship, it is a sort, and there are millions of them on the planet at any point, quite literally. In reality, the causes of the distress, which is so personal and offensive, are general phenomena which have been well studied and mapped by sober laboratory researchers. As always, the answer is simply information. There is an important difference between acting on our evasive or nervous urges – and knowing that one has them, realizing where they have come from and discussing why they make us do what we do, is preferable. We can't – most of us – be entirely safe in love, but we can almost be as beneficial: we can develop into people who are committed to understanding our dysfunctional trauma-driven actions in due time before we get too angry and harm other individuals too much. There are few things that are more beautiful than a couple who have learned to tell each other with maturity and patience that they have been triggered in an obvious or nervous way, but do whatever they can to get things right – and hope that in a while they will be fine.

HOW TO DEAL WITH FEARFUL-AVOIDANT ATTACHMENT.

It might be difficult to say if you are afraid and avoidable without consulting a specialist. Although you can take an online test to decide your attachment style, you cannot clearly differentiate between the two other attachment types because the former is so unusual and in reality, a mixture of the other two.

In any case, take a deep breath if you contribute to all of the above and feel anxious. The good news is that attachment forms can be combined and adapted through deliberate intention and practice. You can change the theme of your connection. This is how to get things moving if you have a frightening-avoiding attachment:

Any things you can do here:

Recognize that your feelings might not give you exact input about what is happening in your relationships.

The difficulty you feel may have nothing to do with your present romantic partner or close friend. Think of it as a post-traumatic stress response.

Try seeing a therapist or using an auto support service such as Adult Alcoholics Children or Co-Dependents Anonymous to share your true feelings and experiences in a safe environment (no matter how off) to get a supportive viewpoint to calibrate your emotional and behavioral responses better. People with fearful attachment styles frequently do not know how to feel or react in situations of emotional distress.

Take a long time (maybe days) before you act on strong emotions. Make sure you have all the facts on the table and decide how to react before you take action.

Practice setting healthy boundaries.
Perhaps during your childhood, you didn't have clear boundaries, which does not come naturally. When in a relaxed emotional environment, ask yourself what you need in your relationships and what habits, then communicate this

knowledge openly in a non-defensive fashion. Of course, you should note that you do not feel comfortable under any other adult's power to "create." This is your job. This is your work.

Don't disclose too much of your inner turmoil or trauma history until you know that the listener is "safe."
The vulnerability you feel when revealing it too quickly may overwhelm you with intense anxiety that causes you to flee and disrupt your relationship. I also try to slow down my work with stressful people if they want to share their closest secrets too early in the therapeutic relationship. I ask them why they feel that I can trust their well-being. I think I am trustworthy, but I want people to determine when and how their defenses are reduced by themselves.

Practice standing your ground, not running away, and experiencing healthy endings.
I always recommend to my clients that we know when we have a near therapeutic relationship, so they are afraid to come to their appointments and worry about excuses not to come. This also refers to friendships and relationships. If you are like this, simply expect this emotional response and fail to do so when it is said to you (of course, do not disregard the indicators of possible violence or inappropriate behavior). If you are told how much they care for, you should also be compelled to embrace the gesture graciously. Know, when you encourage others to show their own good, you give them a gift. Finally, strive to remain until the end of the partnership. There is no friendship forever. Like the tide, they ebb and flow. Listen to the other, speak the truth and release them when it is time for a

relationship to end. Don't worry; you're really going to have to love yourself.

Develop a mindfulness practice.

It is crucial for you to understand why your choices surrounding your sex life and relationships are a good way to develop self-awareness – the practice of being present and conscious of your emotions.

"In our relationship, switching from reactivity to reactivity will lift us from our early attachments to healthier, safer style," writes Linda Carroll, M.S. licensed marriage therapist and family therapist at Mbg. "Every time you feel like your partner is getting too close or too far away, listen to both of you and what they and how they say it. You may find that in emotional circumstances, your words cause a physiological response of struggle or flight.

Be honest with your partners.

If you want actually to form a near emotional connection with someone, you will have to explain exactly what you want and why you compete with them. In this way, you can also focus on ways to resolve and get closer to your challenges.

"There's no point in pretending to be more ready than you are for love, cuddles and almsgiving, and you should be frank about your own relationship form and what it entails. After all, you want to meet someone who embraces your attachments and is as happy as you are.

Get real about self-compassion.

This isn't just a good feeling for you. At heart, people with defiant, evasive personalities have a relationship insecurity — an instilled confidence that, as your earliest parents or relatives did, people in your life would fail or abandon you. You must work diligently to crack the negative mentality that is unacceptable for you because of what happened in your past.

"The fact is that nobody can fix your attachment problems," couple psychologist Margaret Paul, Ph.D., says mbg. "True healing comes when you learn to be the caring parent you never had to yourself. How did you harm your childhood? How do you give yourself the comfort, support and affirmation you have never had?"

In the end, sex with many people and the enjoyment of freedom is nothing wrong — if it comes from a safe place and serves a healthy function. Your sex life should feed you if you're looking for physical pleasures, news or emotional connection.

Challenge the lens through which you process relational data.

Just because you interpret an event or declaration in one way does not mean that it is a fact. If we have faith in something, we always search for evidence to reinforce our trust. If we have numerous negative and pessimistic assumptions about relationships, we will find evidence to support our findings. When you meet anyone, for example, you may find out that they broke up with their last partner and that they would reject you, you assume. Or if they haven't written to you all day long, you assume they can't love you, or they can't care about you.

We prefer to look for facts to validate our convictions. While in some cases, it can be beneficial, it may also be very harmful. It is also important to be mindful of how you manage details and knowledge about your partner and your relationship. You may internalize this view and create negative confidence in distorted or incomplete knowledge.

If you read this and wonder who knows who this style is, you should realize that you will not see it until you get close and have an intimate attitude with the guy. You may also see that the individual is dysregulated and disorganized if his or her personal safety is endangered because of things like serious illness, bullying and job loss.

It is also important to remember that even though you have stable styles of attachment from your childhood, this style can go down to a terrifying style though you subsequently suffer a significant loss such as the death of a parent or are otherwise traumatized (e.g. violent crime, assault, or a long-term emotional abuse). Be careful if you are in relation to someone like this. Realize that you can not take away all the suffering. You should be there for them and provide encouragement and support when pursuing their own inner work. If you want to remain in the relationship, you should know that you will still be exposed to "testing behaviors." If you're scared, you may have some unpleasant or complicated behaviors to see whether you are going to reject them or injure them. After all, their training has taught them to expect that. However, if you take thisbehavior, and do not take them too personally, I know, easier said than done, the individual will probably start to control their emotions efficiently and be much more comfortable with the intimacy of their relationships.

REWIRING YOUR AVOIDANT, ANXIOUS, OR FEARFUL ATTACHMENT STYLE

The best thing to do with your relationships is to improve your relationship with you.

Now what? What? People can readily see aspects of their styles that are maladaptive and cause relationship issues. In order to help people adjust, make up for and deal with their attachment styles I am going to discuss below, how to:

- • Dealing with and using feelings as data

- • Accept the actions of other people

- • Pick more welcoming environments

- • Refrain from being hijacked emotionally

I can now give you some ways of reworking your relational structure and modifying your scheme or roadmaps for what you intend to happen in relation to other people (i.e., type of attachment).

To make the most of this topic, we must first cover some material on the functioning of the brain. Have you ever learned that only 10% of our brains are used? Okay, that's clearly wrong. Much of the time, we use all our minds. What the argument actually means is that our minds are very little, specifically involved in what we consider to be a conscious thought. Much of our brain functions are unconscious and are performed below the consciousness level. For instance, if you jump a ball, your hand will automatically rise to catch or block a ball, without having to plan the movement consciously.

The physiological components of the emotional systems often work below the consciousness level. Most of the human emotions are regulated by a brain region known as the limbic system. Amygdala is one of the key mechanisms involved in emotional responses, attachment processes and emotional memories.

WE CAN USE OUR KNOWLEDGE OF HOW THE AMYGDALA WORKS TO SHAPE OUR OWN PERSONALITIES.

The amygdala is an automated cognitive generator and storage facility. As knowledge arrives from your senses into your brain, it enters a relay station called the thalamus. The thalamus sends these details to two locations: to the cortex for conscious analysis (i.e., you can think about what happened) and directly to the amygdala to rapidly decide if the incoming information is a danger. The amygdala is a "dirty" conduit. Its principal role is to determine yes/no: threats or no threats. And depending on your attachment style, and the vulnerability of your childhood emotional system, a possible loss of work, actual physical attacks, raised voices, possibly dismissal of facial expressions or even items so subtle that you are not aware of them may be a threat.

Regardless of the origin, once a threat is detected, the amygdala triggers the release of adrenaline. The amygdala can cause a discharge of adrenaline before the cortex can even actively comprehend what happened. The cortex then decides the essence of the threat and whether it accepts that the action is justified, sends the amygdala a second message that there is a danger.

EVEN WITHOUT AN EXTERNAL TRIGGER, YOUR CORTEX CAN SEND THREAT SIGNALS TO YOUR AMYGDALA.

Most of us can remember memories that are painful or upsetting, or we can imagine circumstances that cause an emotional reaction. In this situation, we have an emotional response to a recollection or perceived occurrence that is not real. Some of us have even dreamed of success or love or other encounters that can carry positive emotions. The argument here is that input data are receptive to our emotional processes, but they don't care where the data comes from (real circumstance or imagination). You can deliberately change emotional experiences with the use of your imagination and your speech and words.

IMAGINED EVENTS CAN RESULT IN THE CREATION OF NEW POSITIVE MEMORIES.

Take a moment to imagine a fantasy you had in the past for some time. You have a recollection of an extraordinary occurrence. You dreamed of it literally. Taken together with our discussion of emotions, you may consciously create new memories along with relevant emotions.

Fresh memories and feelings rewire the brain literally. The brain is very versatile. The ties you use are improved a lot. Those you don't need are damaged and pruned down. Thus, if you're caught in a loop of remembering traumatic memories or imagining anxiety or heartbreaking experiences, these circuits are readily developed and activated.

This pattern must be reversed by increasing the positive trajectories and weakening the pessimistic, nervous pathways. Repeated positive thinking, along with positive feelings, creates new memories and stimulates pleasure centers in your brain.

CHANGE IS NOT EASY. IT INVOLVES SUSTAINED REGULAR PRACTICE.

Here are some ideas:

1. Write positive affirmation cards on 3x5 index cards. Read them to yourself (preferably out loud) as often as possible.

A positive statement is a simple, optimistic statement like "I'm lovable" or "I'm a worthy individual." At first, it does not matter whether or not you believe it.

If you're like many people, for years you've had a steady stream of depressive thoughts. These derogatory "tapes" act like noise in the background. You will easily record a new tape by reading your confirmation cards regularly.

If you don't accept that repetition contributes to the recording of new tracks, consider this: I can sing a commercial Pepsi song word for word from 1976. I recite the commercial word for word Life Cereal ("Hey Mikey!"). Why are these advertisements in my mind continuously emblazoned, even though I never tried to remember them? One explanation: repetition. One explanation. It's time for a new jingle to record!

2. Learn to talk to yourself and be your own positive motivational coach.

For years, many of us have attacked ourselves without restraint. When you do this, you are reinforcing negative directions that trigger anxiety. You absolutely have to continue to judge yourself. Don't worry; you'll be overcorrected and become a deluded narcissist. And without your help, the world is cruel enough.

"Nobody knows how stressed I'm" or "I'm going to do fine." Researchers have found that people who are high-powered and optimistic about the future use positive self-talk when engaged in tough tasks.

Learn to speak for yourself. Believe it or not, a lot of people say they don't think in words. You may need to know how to speak to yourself as you want to control your emotions and think consciously. Here's an instrument:

Move narrated. Start as long as you're still at home. Say all (if you can) you see and experience: "I get up and walk to the entrance. One step, two steps, three steps, four. I'm placing the doorknob with my ear. It's cold. It's cold. I walk outside. I step outside. It's warm, but still quite chilly ...

3. Do mirror work.

Go to space where you have fair privacy standards. Look in the mirror at yourself. Look right in your eyes and say, "I love you," as sincerely as you can.

I could not maintain a straight face or keep from laughing the first time I did. Now, with absolute honesty, I can look into my own eyes and make it feel totally warm and perfect.

Say it. Do it. Note, your emotional system knows only incoming information. He doesn't know where the data comes. Your emotional system will know that someone is looking at you and saying, "I love you."

People respond to this task in different ways, and I have some customers who can never do it. But look at it like this: if it's pointless and dumb, why would it be so difficult for you to do it?

4. Do imaginal inner child work using creative visualization.

Many with stable types have a warehouse of memories of people who are there to help and encourage them. In short, these memories combine to create an "internalized, stable core." In mild to moderately distressing times, stable people should not reach out to a real individual. You can affirm and reassure yourself, control your own feelings and get yourself moving again. If you are one of 45 percent who hasn't had enough stable childhood memories, you can now build some new memories. Of course, if you happen to be in your life, you can use a genuinely stable person as the foundation. But if not, all you've got is yourself. And that's good enough. That's good enough.

Get warm, calm and ready to meditate shortly. Open your eyes. Shut your eyes. Imagine you being a young kid. It also helps to see your child playing in a meadow outside. Present yourself as the future. Tell the child you made it. Tell the kid. You grow up. You grew up. Then tell the child you came to love them. You're still going to be there for them. You're never going to leave them. Hear how the child replies. If the child is going to let you (and they might not), hug them. And don't give up if it doesn't work the first time! Keep coming back. Keep coming back. After all, you vowed to be there always. This is just a taste of the imaginative activities that you can perform.

Responding to Your Partner's Attachment Style

Are You Too Attached or Detached?

The Golden Rule is definitely good advice on social interactions. It encourages us to put ourselves in the shoes of others and imagine how we feel. When I fail to get dry cleaning from work on my way home, I want my wife to understand, not to be scornful. And so, I should be patient when she comes through the door without the suit I wanted to wear tomorrow, and not get angry. Empathy also teaches us how to treat others.

The explanation that the Golden Rule works, in general, is because we are all in many respects the same. We have the same basic needs for love and acceptance, and like everyone else, we experience the same happiness and sorrow, terror and disappointment. How we feel in a given situation is also very definitely how other people feel. However, there are also situations where we don't all have the same requirements and emotions, and the Golden Rule can lead us terribly distracted in

122

these situations. The attachment styles in intimate relationships are one example.

FORMING EMOTIONAL BONDS

Attachment is the deep emotional connection that forms in the first weeks and months of life between a child and a mother (or another caregiver). If children are firmly attached to their mothers, they use them to discover the world from a stable foundation. But the infant retreats to his mother at the first sign of threat who offers physical support and emotional assistance.

Around two-thirds of Americans' children are firmly attached and the majority of them who are insecurely linked fall into two types: children who are eventually attached feel that they cannot trust their caregiver to console them so that they can learn to relax themselves instead. Instead, anxiously attached children discover that when they are fussy enough, they will catch the attention of the caregiver.

In early childhood, our attachment styles become a functioning model of relationships that lead us through our relationships with friends and others for the rest of our lives. This working model consists of two components: one is a measure of how many others are important, namely, whether or not they can be trusted to support them when appropriate. The other is a self-model; that is, how possible it is that you will fulfil your needs and are even deserving of this assistance.

MISMATCHED ATTACHMENT STYLES

When two firmly attached adults enter into an intimate relationship, their models intuitively direct them to find and provide physical comfort and emotional support when necessary. The Golden Rule works for these lucky couples. However, when attachment patterns do not fit, relationship issues are unavoidable.

In a recent article on the Latest Opinion on Psychology, as psychologists Jeffry Simpson and Steven Rholes point out, attachment behavior is not universal instructions to discuss interpersonal contact. Rather, in relationships, they are ways to cope with tension.

When times are good, such as the beginnings of new love, partners' types of attachment cannot be evident. Often when a pair experiences a traumatic occurrence — they fail to call, do not respond to a text message instantly, and come late for dinner — do attachments grow.

AVOIDANCE AND ANXIETY

Two forms of attachment conduct are described by Simpson and Rholes:

Avoidance: This refers to the warmth of a person in a relationship of emotional intimacy. People who are highly vulnerable to avoidance are finding power through self-confidence and autonomy. In times of tension, they retire and seek solace in solitude.

Anxiety: This refers to how often a person is worried that a partner will give up or fail them. They invest heavily in the relationship, but continuously doubt the commitment of their partner because they feel unworthy. Its commitment also pushes its partner away, enhancing its insecurities only.

Notice that these are not definitions but lengths, so that you or your partner can stop it or think about it to different degrees. Individuals with low dimensions are considered firmly attached. They seek support through physical closeness and open-mindedness and the devotion of their partner to the relationship is evident, because they believe they are deserving and deserving of it.

PARTNER BUFFERING

Although attachment patterns are set in the first year of life, they can shift slowly as people have new knowledge in relationships. A vulnerable or insecure person whose spouse is firmly attached will gradually learn to reduce his insecurities. However, the firmly attached partner needs a lot of experience and determination to make this move. You need much more reassurance from your nervous partner than you believe appropriate. Often, if they need time and space for themselves, you will need to learn not to disturb your avoiding partner.

Simpson and Rholes name the buffering of this process partner. In other words, you respond to your significant other in a way that suits their style of attachment. If you do this, the pain of your partner is alleviated, and the tension in the relationship can be resolved.

So, if your nervous wife needs a telephone call, even though you are only a few minutes late, always make the call. She will respond more to your needs if her problems are alleviated. Or if your obvious husband retreats to his man's cavern, let him be —

but carry his meals to him, so he knows you're concerned still. If he thinks he can withdraw when he is tired, he would be more relaxed to open at other times.

You may think that partner buffering promotes bad behavior, rewards an insecure commitment to attachment or facilitates isolation by more space. Reward and punishment can form basic behaviors effectively.

But attachment is not a simple habit: a dynamic network of cognitions and actions, a system of relationships, essential others and oneself. You may support your avoiding or nervous partner over time, but you need to expand on what already exists and not knock it down and start again.

ACTING AGAINST YOUR INTUITION

Partner buffering requires intense self-consciousness and a readiness to work against your intuitions at some times. This is particularly true with regard to the relationship between avoidants and nervous people. In order to buffer your partner, you have to take a close look first, before you recognize your own types of attachment and those of your partner clearly. And then you must commit to buffering, let your aim and not your intuition be your guide.

You will have to maintain your attachment and confidence, if you are nervous, that your partner is genuinely committed and that you are deserving of this commitment. And do not follow it by any means when your partner retreats. You might have to provide more emotional support than you feel comfortable with if you are the avoidant. And don't withdraw when your partner pursues, but sit there and offer all the reassurance he or she wants.

Intimate partnerships all include meeting the needs of each other. But following the Golden Rule to consider the needs of our partner may confuse us. Instead of giving our important people what we want ourselves, we must give them what they want. And they will feel comfortable enough to fulfil our own needs when we fulfil them.

ARE YOU FEELING INSECURE?

One of the greatest problems in which I see people fight is fear. This is mainly why I have devoted a great deal of my life to researching self-conscious thinking and perceptions with "conscious inner voices." It's not shocking that one of the most common self-attacks I have seen recorded in decades of study is, I'm different from everyone else. "It's incredible to feel left out and low about ourselves, with studies estimating that 85 % of people suffer from little self-esteem. Those of us who feel insecure may feel isolated, but we are in the majority.

One of the issues I have been grappling with in recent times is how current events influence the sense of self. Insecurity may be compounded when people spend a lot of time in their minds and alone. The longer they are alone, the more they slip into fear for others who feel uncomfortable about social or personal experiences. While our situations can be different, the ways to understand and resolve fear are the same. My approach to uncertainty mainly includes discussing two key concepts: the theory of attachment and the theory of separation.

ATTACHMENT THEORY AND INSECURITY

Our experience of attachment plays a significant role in the degree of comfort we feel in life, in our relationships and within ourselves. The early patterns of connection that we had with our primary caregivers serve as a blueprint for how we expect relationships to function throughout our lives and inform our sense of identity. We are firmly attached to them if we feel protected, soothed, and seen by our parents or caretakers. However, if our parents can't cope with us and fix relationship fractures, we can build an unsecured attachment pattern. In infancy, the habits of unstable attachment are nervous and Anxious attachment, anxiously resisting attachment and disorganized attachment.

A child with an anxious-Anxious relationship can have an irregular parent who is more emotional than caring. The child will adapt by turning the volume on its needs and focusing on the parent. They try to get the parent's needs by grasping, screaming, or ordering. Since the parent is there emotionally sometimes and sometimes not, the child feels anxious, much as the parent wants to care about them, this pattern leaves a person uncertain whether they can rely on others. They internalize a feeling of fear and depression. As adults, you prefer to seek partners that are emotionally unreliable and circumstances in which you sometimes feel hurt, and while this is difficult, your inner working model is familiar to you and confirms how others treat you. People also contribute to this process by continuous reassurance by seeking attention from their partners.

A child develops an evasive relationship if a parent is unable to fulfil their needs and emotionally inaccessible. The child adapts to escape the traumatic experience of voicing a need and having nobody respond by suppressing knowledge of their own needs. Since the child can't afford to see the parent as faulty and lose its protection, it falls like they don't matter, which is disgraceful. The child learns to control himself and to be self-parent. They will then grow up to feel pseudo-independent and burdened by other people's needs. They always look for a partner with "healthy" feelings and anxiety needs. This choice increases their internalized understanding of the need for them to take care of themselves and of the need for others who express themselves. However, an avoidant is always dangerous when he or she feels overwhelmed and cannot continue the attempt to ignore his or her needs.

A child develops a disorganized relationship when a parent is frightened of them or when the child is frightened or confused and scared. Such a parent induces uncertainty without a solution. The child wants to go to them for protection, but when they're near, they have to run. This leaves a child without a coordinated plan to meet its needs. As a result, they build the fear of others internalizing and at the same time, the fear of being without other people. Their insecurities can feel daunting because they are traumatic.

These unstable attachment patterns, developed in our first relationships, often manifest in an unsafe adult attachment that especially affects our romantic relations and the parenthood but also informs how we feel. If we are more convinced to understand our fear individually, we must be prepared to go back to our history of attachment, which gives us vital clues as to why we believe, feels, and acts in our way of doing things, why we remain unsafe and why we constantly put ourselves and our needs into a negative light.

SEPARATION THEORY AND INSECURITY

My father, psychologist and author Robert Firestone, developed separation theory. The theory shows how traumatic early childhood experiences, in conjunction with existential consciousness, lead people to psychological defenses. Defenses that suit real situations, e.g. denial, neglect, emotional deprivation, or harassment of a parent, which originally harmed a person's self, continue to harm or restrict the sense of self throughout their lives.

A child internalizes the negative attitudes of its parents to them and the complicated ways parents view themselves. Since a young child depends on the parent for survival, it feels too unsafe to break away from the perspective of the parent or to see shortcomings of the parent. Rather, children internalize negative behaviors and values of their parents as their own. For example, the child can see himself as unwanted or unlovable if a parent is misplaced or unavailable. If a kid responds as if he is too loud or insecure, he may see himself as an odd or burden.

A child's negative core beliefs form an inner dialogue, known as the essential internal voice. This "voice" becomes a lifelong critique, perpetuating most of his vulnerability. As we walk through various stages of life, we feel this filter. The critical inner voice adds to certain negative characteristics that suit an early self-image. When we pursue a relationship, our inner critic will say, "You're never going to find someone who loves you. If we become parents, it may say, "You can't deal with this. You 're too unattracted / bound / unsecure / unworthy / unworthy." When it comes to our jobs or aspirations, you can tell us "You're not talented/capable/smart/noticeable." You're a horrible mother/father.

Even when it is a pandemic, the voice will reach us with a broad range of attacks that intensify our struggles. "You don't know what you are doing, what you are doing. You're not at this. Your children hate you. Your children hate you. You'll lose your job. You will always be lonely. You'll mess up and get sick. Whatever the situation we are in and whatever we say to you, it is worth remembering that the critical inner voice is the core feelings we have experienced or witnessed in ways that affect us very early in our lives. If we are to reinforce and go beyond these old beliefs, we have to consider and question them and how they are woven into our sense of self.

Looking at our history will help us shed light on our negative conception of ourselves. Knowing the root of our vulnerability will motivate us from the ground up to question them.

THE SECURE ATTACHMENT STYLE

A stable attachment connection that meets a child's need for stability, calmness and understanding enables the child's nervous system to grow optimally.

A child's brain grows to provide a framework that relies on a sense of protection.

Still, wonder why other people have different approaches to relationships? Or why do certain people still seem to be facing the same issues, no matter who they are from?

This is possibly due to their form of attachment.

We learn our types of attachment as children from our parents. But when we grow older, we still display these relationship patterns unless we make a concerted effort to change them.

Experiencing trauma in children or coming home to a traumatic situation can contribute, for example, to preventative, Anxious or disorganized types of attachment. That being said, even those with relatively idyllic families may have formed relational dynamics, which are evasive, Anxious or disorderly. In my previous blog posts, you can learn all about these kinds of attachments.

On the other hand, people who feel a sense of security at home and love their parents are usually more likely to exemplify the stable type of attachment. However, those with less healthy children may have often learned to develop safe relationships through their own intensely introspective practice. The argument is that, instead of merely believing that someone is not capable of secure a relationship based on your understanding of its history, you have the opportunity to understand who you are dealing with.

WHAT IS SECURE ATTACHMENT AND BONDING?

Although establishing a healthy fastening relationship with a child is simpler, it can be formed at any age – and your child can make the best possible start in life.

The bond between a child and you, your parent or primary caregiver, is the emotional connection. A key study, released by the Early Childhood Development Science Committee in 2000, identified how important the bonding connection is to the development of an infant. This mode of communication influences the mental, physical, intellectual, emotional and social growth of your child. Indeed, the strength of this relationship is the primary indicator of your child's success in school and in life.

The attachment relationship is not based on the quality of your care or parental affection, but on nonverbal emotional contact with your child. Although attachments arise when you are, the parent or caregiver, caring for the needs of your baby varies the consistency of the attachment.

A strong attachment bond ensures your child is healthy, understood and comfortable enough to experience optimal nervous system growth. The growing brain of your child organizes itself to provide the best framework for life for your child: a sense of security that contributes to an effort to learn, healthy self-confidence, trust and empathy.

An unstable attachment relationship does not fulfil the need for stability, understanding and calmness in your child, which prevents the child from developing a brain in the best possible way. This can hinder social, mental and even physical growth, which contribute to learning difficulties and relationship-building in later life.

HOW SECURE ATTACHMENT IS CREATED

You do not need to build a safe connection between you and your child and give your child the best start in life. The 2000 study found that the crucial aspect of the relationship between child and primary caregiver is NOT based on the standard of treatment, educational experience or even the bond of love between the parent and the infant. It is focused instead on the quality of the nonverbal contact between you and your child.

If a child is still an infant and relying on nonverbal means of communication, it is easier to develop a healthy bond, so you can begin to make your child feel understood and comfortable at any age. The brains of children begin to mature long into adulthood (until the mid-20s). Moreover, it's never too late to initiate a nonverbal emotional interaction with your child because the brain keeps developing over the lifetime. Developing your nonverbal communication skills will potentially help strengthen and deepen your relationships with others of all ages.

The bond of attachment varies from the bond of affection

As your child's parent or primary caregiver, you can obey all conventional parenting rules, provide your baby with care 24 hours a day, and yet do not firmly bind. You can take care of every physical need of your child, have the most comfortable home, food of the highest quality, the best training and all the things that a child would want. You can keep, cuddle and enjoy your child without forming the kind of relationship that encourages your child's best growth. How can this be? It is necessary to establish a secure bond of attachment, rather than to establish a bond of love.

Children need more than love and care to grow their brains and nervous systems in the best possible way. Children must be able to interact with their primary caregiver in non-verbal emotional communication, so that they express their desires and feel heard, safe and healthy. Children who feel emotionally distant from their primary caregiver may feel confused, frustrated, and unsure regardless of how much they are loved.

THE DIFFERENCE BETWEEN BONDING AND A SECURE ATTACHMENT BOND

Bonding	Secure Attachment Bond
Refers to your feelings for and sense of connection to your child that begins before birth and usually develops very quickly in the first weeks after	Refers to your child's emotional connection with you (their primary caregiver) that begins at birth, develops rapidly in the next two years and continues developing

the baby is born.	throughout life.
Is task-oriented. You attend to your child's needs, whether it's changing diapers and feeding, or taking to soccer practice and the movies.	Requires you to focus on what is happening at the moment between you and your child. Your child's nonverbal cues tell you that they feel unhappy, for example, and you respond wordlessly by mirroring your child's expression to show you understand and then giving your child a hug.
You keep your adult speed regularly while you look after your boy. For instance, you are eager to feed your kid's dinner so that you can watch your favorite TV show or cut short playing a game with your kid to answer the text.	You follow the slower pace of your child and take the time to decode and answer nonverbal signs of your child that interact, for example, "I'm no fast rush, I'm just having fun with you."
As a parent, you start communicating with your kids. You want to take, for example, a nice picture of your baby laughing, so you start playing or give your teen his favorite meal, so he's going to tell you how things go at school.	Your child begins and finishes your relationship. You take nonverbal signs from your kid, so you delay taking a cute shot. Or take up the teenage questions that aren't a good time to address and delay the questions.
For example, you concentrate	You just concentrate on the

on future goals by trying to do what you can to get the best, healthiest kid.	moment-to-moment experience and just enjoy connecting to your kids. You listen, chat or play with your child and offer your absolute, concentrated attention in ways that feel comfortable with him or her so that you can live "at the moment."

WHY THERE IS SO MUCH CONFUSION ABOUT BONDING AND THE SECURE ATTACHMENT BOND?

Binding or binding are also used to describe both caring and emotional communication, but they are very different methods of communicating with your child.

This is a relationship based on parent caring for his child, while the other is focused on the quality of nonverbal emotional contact between the parent and the infant.

Both kinds of interaction between parent and child can occur at the same time. You can also create the emotional bond while eating, bathing or otherwise caring for your child by identifying and reacting to nonverbal signs of your child.

Until researchers recognized the profound changes in the infant's brain during the first months and years of their lives, the pattern of treatment and attachment appeared quite familiar. Now, however, they may identify and carefully monitor nonverbal reactions of children to reinforce the attachment process in infants.

DEVELOPMENTAL MILESTONES RELATED TO SECURE ATTACHMENT

In recognizing the developmental milestones of healthy attachment, you can identify and quickly repair signs of unsecured attachment. It is important to contact your pediatrician or child development specialist if your child fails certain milestones.

From birth to 3 months, your infant ...

Following colors, movement and objects and responding to them?

Shift to sounds? Sounds switch?

Display interest in looking at the faces of people?

When you smile, smile back?

Between three and six months, your kid ...

Show joy when you interact?

Make sounds, such as cooing, babbling and crying, happy or unhappy?

At playtime, smile a lot?

From 4 to 10 months, your baby does ...

Do facial gestures and sounds like laughing, giggling or babbling interact?

Have you had playful exchanges?

Are the movements (giving and taking), the sounds and the smiles alternating?

From 10 to 18 months, your baby ...

Play games like a peek-a-boo or a patty cake with you?

Using ma, ba, pa, da, ga sounds?

Use various movements (sometimes one by one) to display needs like waving, giving or pointing?

When named, remember his or her name?

Does your baby between 18 and 20 months ...

At least ten terms know and understand?

Using in words or babbling, at least four consonants, such as b, d, m, n, p, t?

Using words, movements and signs to convey needs, such as pointing to something that will take you to?

Enjoy easy games such as kissing or feeding a doll or a stuffed animal?

Demonstrate familiarity with persons or body parts when they are named?

Do your baby at 24 months ...

At least 50 terms know and understand?

Using two or more words together, like "want milk" or "more crackers? Show more complex games, like feeding the stuffed animal and positioning the animal in the scooter?

Show interest in playing with other children by giving other children items or toys?

Answer questions about familiars or items did not present while searching for them?

Do your baby at 36 months ...

Set together thoughts and actions, such as 'sleepy, want blankets' or 'yoghurt hungry and go to the fridge?'

Enjoy playing with kids and talking to other adults? Speak about emotions and desires, and showtime (past and future) knowledge?

Answer the questions without too much difficulty "who," "when," "when" and "where?"

Pretend to play various characters — by dressing and acting, or with toy figures or dolls?

OBSTACLES TO CREATING A SECURE ATTACHMENT BOND

Barriers to a secure connection can occur when your child is an infant. You may love your baby deeply but are not prepared to meet the needs of the immature nervous system of your child. Since children cannot control themselves and relax, they depend on you to do so. However, if you cannot handle your own tension, regain calmness and concentration quickly in the face of everyday stressors, you will not be able to soothe and calm your child.

Even an old child looks to you, the mom, as a stable and secure connection and eventually. However, if you are often depressed, anxious, frustrated, sad, distracted or negative, your child can suffer from physical, emotional and/or intellectual developments.

The emerging area of infant mental health, with its focus on brain science and parents' developmental function, offers a better understanding of factors that may influence healthy bonding. If either the primary caregiver or the child has a health condition, nonverbal contact between the two may be compromised, and the stable attachment relationship could be impaired.

HOW AN INFANT'S WELL-BEING CAN AFFECT THE SECURE ATTACHMENT BOND

Experience shapes the brain, and this is true, particularly for newborns with relatively undeveloped nervous systems.

When a baby has problems in the womb or in the delivery phase — for example during a cesarean birth — the nervous system may be damaged.

Adopted babies or those who spend time away from a parent in neonatal hospitals may have the early experience, which makes them feel overwhelmed, confused and unsafe.

Children who never seem to stop crying — whose eyes are still closely closed, their fist clenched and their bodies rigid — will find it difficult even to meet a well-adjusted caregiver.

Fortunately, because the infant brain is so underdeveloped and affected by the experience, a child may solve birth problems. It may take a few months, but when the primary caregiver remains calm, concentrated, compassionate and diligent, a child gradually can relax enough to establish a stable attachment phase.

How an older child's well-being can affect the secure attachment bond

The history and atmosphere of a child can influence the ability to establish a secure bond. Sometimes the conditions affecting the secure attachment relationships are inevitable, but the child is too young to understand what happened and why. It actually feels like no one cares for a child, and it loses faith in others and makes the world an unsafe place.

A child only gains attention by acting out or exhibiting such drastic behaviors.

Often the needs of the child are fulfilled and sometimes not. The child doesn't know what to expect.

An infant is either hospitalized or is split from its parents.

An infant is passed from one caregiver to another (which may be the product of pregnancy, parenting, or loss).

A child is mistreated or abused.

How the well-being of a caretaker can affect the safe link

The emotions you feel as a primary caretaker will influence your child's development process. If you are excessively stressed, depressed, traumatized or inaccessible, you may not be conscious or receptive of the constructive emotional input your child needs in order to maintain a stable connection.

Even a safe, loving, and conscientious caregiver will often have difficulties understanding and maintaining a stable link to his child. If you have been a kid without a stable relationship with your own primary caregiver, you do not know what a secure attachment looks like or feels like. However, adults can also improve for the better. Just as exercise and a balanced diet will improve yourself, you can also learn to cope with excessive tension and feelings that can hinder your ability to build a stable connection.

Distractions of daily life

Cell phones, computers, television and many other everyday distractions will keep you from giving your child your full attention. Responding to a pressing e-mail while eating, texting a friend during playtime or just zoning in front of your child's TV are ways parents can lose the opportunity to make eye contact and participate in a healthy bonding phase with their child. You'll miss your child's nonverbal signals without eye contact and full attention

NONVERBAL COMMUNICATION TIPS FOR SECURE ATTACHMENT

Nonverbal signals are sensory signals that interact with a certain tone of voice, contact or face. The primary caregiver of a child puts together all these unrivalled qualities to make a child feel heard, secure and relaxed. Even if a child is old enough to communicate, nonverbal communication remains the key to establishing a safe bond.

Using Nonverbal Communication to Create a Secure Attachment Bond

Your eye contact – You look at your child affectionately, and they feel secure, relaxed and happy about the positive emotion expressed by the nonverbal signal. You might not look directly into your child's eyes if you're sad, anxious or distracted. Maintaining eye contact is also vital to help the flow of communication between you and your child.

Facial Expression – without a word, the face can convey countless emotions. If you interact calmly and attentively with your kids, they're healthy. However, if your face looks upset, frustrated, concerned, sad, scared, or distracted, your child will catch up with these negative emotions.

The tone of speech – While your child is too young to understand your language, he/she will understand the difference between a harsh, dismissive, or worried tone and a tone that transmits tenderness, interest, concern, and understanding. Make sure the sound you use suits what you mean when you speak to older children.

Touch – your child's way of touch transmits your emotional status – whether affection, calmness, tenderness, comfort or disinterest, irritated or not. You can add so much joy to your child by bathing, raising or carrying a baby or by giving your older child a soft, gentle touch on the arm.

Body language – the way you sit, shift and transport yourself provides your child with a wealth of information. Talkback to your child with your arms and head crossed, and they will view you as protective and unselfish. But sit down with a relaxed, open stance, leaning on your child, and you'll feel what they say to you.

Pacing, timing, and intensity – your voice, movement and facial expressions will represent your state of mind in rhythm, timing and intensity. If you maintain a pace for the parent or are anxious or otherwise unaware, your nonverbal acts do little to soothe, encourage or educate your child. You must be mindful of the needs of your child for speed and strength, sometimes slower and less intense than your own.

MOVE TOWARDS SECURE ATTACHMENT

The good news is that you can switch from style to style. Specifically, a better attachment design can be achieved.

Now, it's not a simple or a fast operation, as you might expect. Like any significant shift where you want to modify such a profoundly rooted mind, you have to achieve a strong will.

The first move is to become conscious of your form of attachment. The next step is to want to shift your appropriate style towards a safer style.

If someone with an anxious or evasive style has a long-term relationship with a stable man, they may become more trustworthy and safer.

Conversely, they may also lead the safe individual to their attachment style. You must also be aware of your form, and if you want to travel more safely, patience is required.

Therapy is also an alternative. Self-esteem, avoidance of their interactions and compassion are also important for anxious styles.

HOW TO RESTRUCTURE YOUR THOUGHTS

Ready for the way to do it? Here we go:

For the Avoidant Style

As with every form of shift at such a deep level, understanding is the first move. You understand that you have an evasive approach and you know it because of your partner's experiences.

Try to work for mutual cooperation and encouragement. Try to reduce the desire for full control. Enable your partner to do some things that make it hard for you to do.

Don't always dwell on your partner's imperfections. We all have them note that.

Create a list of the things for which your partner is grateful.

Look for a healthy style partner; they'd be nice for you if at all possible.

If you want to end ties before they go too far, you should be aware of this and allow it to continue to grow.

Get used to consider and even instigate physical touch. Tell yourself that having some intimacy is good for you. Intimacy will help you to feel comfortable.

And you can learn over time that it's all right to rely on other people.

For the Anxious Style

The first thing to work on for the nervous style is to learn to communicate better needs. This is a big problem for the troubled style.

In the first place, you would have less anxiety if you express your needs more clearly, which is already a huge victory. You can also help determine if a future partner is right for you.

148

Try to bring your emotions to the surface and, above all, share them with your partner. Note that you normally interact well with secure attachments; this is what you're doing.

For the Anxious-Avoidant Style

The nervous avoider is a very small percentage of the types of attachment. Since this sort appears to be concerned about the relationship AND more or less alone person, the most important thing here is to work hard to understand your actions.

Use the stable attachment components from the nervous tips and prevent the reorganization of your thoughts to function for greater security.

Ask why if you find yourself driving someone away. If you are upset about your partner leaving you, ask yourself again where it comes from. Did they offer you every reason to believe it? There is no clear proof many times. Let yourself calm down in that situation and try not to get upset with it.

For the Secure Style

Since the aim is to move towards a safer type of connection, it doesn't take much to see.

Anything to be mindful of is only that it's "all right." Don't linger if you and your partner don't have a nice spot. If your partner is nervous or avoidable, keep an eye on the fact that these types do not establish characteristics.

WAYS TO CREATE A SECURE ATTACHMENT

We will later share how therapy can help people who have an unsecured attachment style break a negative attachment bond and create a secure attachment bond, but first of all, we will discuss strategies you can use to assist in building a strong, lasting bond.

1. Focus on Healing

Situations and perceptions of childhood that foster insecure attachments often contribute to embarrassment and self-esteem. Living with shame also results in drawbacks, such as self-denial, self-criticism and even self-destruction, when concentrating on someone else's needs. Starting from these problems will help you lay the foundation for the creation of stable attachments.

These feelings and behaviors are typically related to an autonomous, deeply ingrained conviction that a person deserves no happiness or healthy relationships. As such, people with an unstable relationship style are also often to blame themselves for past behaviors. Although healthy guilt can lead to healthier decisions, the shame and self-loathing that often surround an unstable relationship can make a person constantly feel in fear.

A Case Study on Healing

Lisa, a mother of two, is a prime example of how compassion and self-pity can help to create a safe style of attachment. Raised between hot and cold by a mentally ill mother, Amber formed an unstable attachment style early. Her specific style, anxious attachment vulnerability, has made her unstable and codependent in children and adults.

After three marriages that failed, Amber realized something was wrong. She was professional and mother, but she couldn't maintain a healthy romantic relationship. When her last marriage ended in divorce, she fell into a deeper and self-critical depression. She blamed herself for her failed marriages, all great; she eventually saw how she sabotaged each of them. Amber felt like an utter and complete failure.

Amber was struggling to understand why she couldn't maintain a relationship so that her heart was poured out on a coworker-referred therapist. After several weeks of self-reflection and personal work, Amber began to notice that she did not fail. She only formed an unstable relationship and style of attachment.

Although she had played a role in her marriage, Amber knew that even before her first romantic partner, her issues had been present. She began to look into the creation of her first fragile attachment bond in her childhood.

Amber never learns to be in a caring, trusting relationship due to her insecure attachment to her mother. Recognizing this reality helped her transition to healing and acceptance.

Most people wonder how to forgive themselves for past mistakes. Although the self-forgiveness process is a highly personal one, the steps below are a great start:

Ask yourself and your past choices. Were there variables outside of your control involved? Have you done what you felt at the time was best? How do you interpret your actions today differently?

Gain forgiveness. Obtain forgiveness. There are several steps to pardon, including taking responsibility for your actions, apologizing and amending. If you find it difficult to forgive yourself, try to gain your forgiveness by taking these steps. Give yourself a heartfelt apology. You can also apologize and do what you need to help everyone else who may have been upset by your actions. Finally, promise to go forward and do it.

Go forward, not perfection. If this process appears to be easier said than done, use self-compassion practice to help you through the process of healing. A constructive practice by the Nonviolent Communication Organization (NCO) will help to heal embarrassment and to forgive yourself.

2. Build Self-Esteem

Self-forgiveness is a new beginning. When you're no longer trapped in the misery of the past, you can develop yourself. You still have years of negative self-discussion, embarrassment and criticism, so now is the time to turn things around. Below are some realistic ways to develop self-esteem and help you establish a comfortable style of attachment:

Take priority: People who have poor self-esteem prefer to ignore themselves. You may neglect your fitness, hygiene and emotional well-being because you do not feel dignified of self-handling or self-compassion.

If you are used to disregarding your personal needs and wishes, list the things that you have overlooked. Will you go to the dentist? Do you snack on healthy, nutritious foods? Will you want to quit drinking or smoking? When you have a list, devote yourself to coping one by one with these issues and avoid self-pity when you slip into old habits.

The three complimentary diaries: you'll have to start with a blank notebook and a pen or pencil. Every morning, all you have to do is offer three compliments. Looking in a mirror may be part of the process, but a mirror is not necessary if it looks awkward or uncomfortable. The goal here is to remember your positive attributes periodically. You will see yourself in a more optimistic light with this exercise.

Start a new hobby: One of the learning to respect yourself is to find and to try things that you enjoy. If you want to take images, take a picture. Try boating or waterskiing while you're at home on the water.

Practice positive self-talk: people who are safe and confident usually have an uplifting internal conversation. You can. You can, too. This method can be overwhelming for people who have spent their lives filled with negative self-talk and guilt, but it is worth the effort. When you look in the mirror, you should praise yourself and/or keep a list of your performance. The aim is to become your own cheerleader.

When negative thoughts break, make a deliberate effort to battle them positively. You can think, for instance, "I can't do anything right." Respond by saying, "This isn't true; I'm very good at many things."

By battling against negative thoughts and replacing them with positive ones, you build self-esteem and start to develop a healthy style of attachment that will allow you to trust yourself and others.

3. Acknowledge Your Attachment Style
The third and final way to change your attachment form is by addressing the negative aspects of your unsecure attachment design. If you are an anxiously nervous, codependent and too focused on your partner and his / her needs, try to shift your attention toward the inside. By understanding your own desires, self-esteem, and attachment difficulties, you can feel more comfortable, so that you can develop and sustain healthier relationships.

If you're an insecure and tender to shy away from meeting a wife, infant, family member or friend's needs, make a deliberate effort to begin to meet the needs of your loved ones without compromising your own. If you have an urge to step away, understand your feeling and open yourself to someone that you feel secure with. Silence is exacerbating embarrassment, so it is necessary not to keep your feelings intact.

If you are nervous or evasive or are the mixture of nervous-avoidant, you should switch into a safe type of attachment.

It needs self-awareness, persistence and a deep desire to be healthy, but it can be achieved. You will find that the effort you make will give you more accessible, truthful and fulfilling connections.

HOW CAN YOU TELL IF YOUR PARTNER HAS A SECURE ATTACHMENT STYLE?

Here are a few key signs.

They're Not Jealous
Someone with a healthy style of relationship rarely feels jealous of his mate. Eating out with friends, taking a solo trip, or even getting an ex-friendly text on occasion is usually a problem if you talk about someone who's securely attached.

Unless there are signs that your partner is not trustworthy, a securely connected person is not the kind to challenge or use your phone. This does not indicate, however, that they are apathetic.

They're Comfortable Opening Up

An individual who learned a healthy style of attachment was presumably allowed to express their needs instead of ignoring them.

If your partner is safe, they will probably have no trouble telling you what is happening in their lives. And when they need your help, they will also let you know.

They Keep Heated Discussions Civil

Yeah, a couple will disagree from time to time. But even differences will stay polite if you are dating someone with a stable attachment style.

You're not going to be tempted to raise your voice. Your aim is to be heard, to understand and to fix things between you and not simply prove that you are right and wrong. It is much easier for you both to communicate and to feel comfortable.

They're Empathetic

If you tell your tightly connected partner that you have a hard time, they'll be there for you.

They know how to provide you with additional assistance or are willing to inquire if they can provide help while also fulfilling their own needs. And they're not going to make you feel dramatic or safe. They will express empathy and compassion instead.

They Know How to Compromise

Compromise is not a terrifying word for a secure attachment style individual. You have no trouble backtracking and wondering how you two might find a middle ground.

There's an assumption that no one gets what they want. Instead, it is about finding a way to compromise and be satisfied with the outcome for both of you.

They Prefer Real Commitment

This does not necessarily mean that someone with a stable attachment style rushes into a dedicated relationship. Yet they're less likely to face a scenario of "will they won't" for months to come.

Really, they would rather speak frankly about where you are and maybe pick a mark for the sake of clarification.

They Set and Respect Boundaries

The setting of borders is just a natural part of life for those with a stable relationship style. Their parents also stressed the value of this domestically.

They would therefore not hesitate to chat when they need space or tell you when they are bothered by anything. In return, they will realize that it is their job to step back, not push the buttons when you state your own boundaries.

How Your Romantic Attachment Style Can Affect Your Well-Being & Wallet

In today's date, there are a lot of choices for meeting someone. However, according to the theory of attachment, there are only three types of romantic attachment: stable, nervous, and avoidable. One recent research considered the impact of "life outcomes" – like well-being and financial actions – on attachment anxiety and attachment avoidance.

Our attachment style is influenced by our environment, according to attachment theory. A troubling style of attachment is characterized by vulnerability and a lack of faith, while an evasive style is characterized by things like bouncing back fast from a fragment or not getting deeply involved. According to the researchers, avoidance of commitment and fear are seen as 'insecure relations,' and they are seen as the opposite poles of the types.

Linking Attachment Style with Happiness.

The study, which was published by researchers at the University of Arizona last month, gathered answers from university students in romance. Responses to life satisfaction, relationship satisfaction and financial satisfaction have been given.

The data showed that people with attachment disorder also report a lower overall level of life satisfaction, low satisfaction with relationships and little financial satisfaction.

Assembly avoidance was also related to lower life and relation satisfaction, but with financial satisfaction, it did not indicate the same thing. However, the researchers observed that participants with both attachment types appeared to be less financially responsible.

HOW FINANCES ARE AFFECTED BY ATTACHMENT STYLE.

In the case of people with anxiety about commitment, they will attempt to "purchase" their partner's affection for donations. According to Li, "people who are very anxious about attachment can use the money to take care of others."

In comparison, those with evitative attachments may spend their money for their own profit less responsibly.

The researchers conclude that the reasoning behind these actions is based on the features of these attachment types. Many who resist attachment are probably less likely to respect their partner, while vulnerability in relationships can lead to mistrust.

Due to the correlation between finance and well-being, the investigators intend to continue investigating the effect of the style of attachment on financial decision-making.

There is a lot of people that are wrong about the theory of attachment, and if you really want to, you can try to not become like them.

SECURE ATTACHMENT ALLOWS FOR GROWTH AFTER TRAUMA

Childhood is a crucial period to explore and improve secure attachment,preferably established in the early years of a child parental partnership. Our earliest relationships do a lot to build our sense of self and well-being. Knowing that "I matter, my needs matter, and my loved ones will help to keep me safe" reinforces the self-worth of a child.

Safe attachment helps shape a person's awareness of self-care, self-pity and healthy relationships. These are vital to our well-being. The ability to form a healthy bond as an infant offers a cornerstone for lifelong mental wellbeing.

SECURE ATTACHMENT IS A HUMAN NEED

Regrettably, most children do not grow up believing they are seen, loved and embraced.

Many children have unsure, nervous or disorganized forms of attachment. These may lead to negative experiences in childhood (ACEs). This is traumatic and can result in trauma. Children's TV pioneer Fred Rogers cared deeply about the children's feelings of distress.

Mr. Rogers consistently helped spectators – especially children-to, understand the essence of healthy attachment, even without formal training in psychotherapy. His signature PBS series, Neighborhood Mister Rogers, recommended the secure access elements every day — even if they were never used. His programming included compassion, affection, acceptance and appreciation. He informed children that they are precisely valued for who they are – teaching them how to affirm the same for others.

The nature of emotionally stable relationships has been repeatedly described by Fred Rogers for all. It is the sort of relationship that we all need as human beings to flourish and prosper. Anyone can learn to create secure attachment — and at any point in life, it can be created!

"We are all the best opportunities to become the healthiest of people because we know we can be treated just as we are."

POST-TRAUMATIC GROWTH IS POSSIBLE!

Won't you be my friend, the latest documentary film? Shows us a profound post-traumatic example of development. Fred Rogers's own trauma story is exposed, referring to his history of childhood bullying, depression and intense fighting. He suffered unbearable guilt and depression, spent hours in bed and felt alone.

I wonder if Rogers' self-worth messages and the arguments he made with viewers came from his own recovery. I wonder if he might help more children find the acceptance he'd always been looking for. It made me think of 12-step meetings where other people are helped as a part of the healing process. All learn something by helping others. I feel Mr. Rogers has not only demonstrated the framework for stable attachment to many children. His district also enabled him to continue recovering, flourishing, and developing as an individual. It was his own business.

"What is human is listed, and whatever is listed may be more manageable. When we talk about our emotions, they become less stressful, less distressed and less terrifying. The people we trust in this critical discussion will let us realize that we're not alone.

SECURE RELATIONSHIPS NEED NOT BE PERFECT TO BE HEALTHY

I really appreciated how you wouldn't be my neighbor? Rogers' morality depicted. And Mr. Rogers hasn't always been amazing. The film gave his sons the very real view, that with the aura of their dad's sainthood, it was not always easy to grow and that Rogers as a father was not always a saint! No matter how far you go — or how much good you do for others — there is still room for self-pity and development.

"How unfortunate it is that we are surrendering to those who are just like us."

A TRAUMA SURVIVOR'S DEEPENED SENSITIVITY TO OTHERS

People with trauma may feel more vulnerable to others because of what was lacking in their own lives. You can see more clearly the holes in unmet needs. When a trauma victim has been brought out on the other side of a healing path, thriving and prospering, they might be better able to secure connection to others.

"Love and confidence will make a huge difference in the world in the gap between what we said and what we learned in our lives." – Fred Rogers.

DOES AFFIRMING EVERYONE'S VALUE CREATE SELFISH PEOPLE?

One of the complaints from the neighborhood of Mr. Rogers is that it encouraged a generation of greedy people who heard that you are unique and special! I disagree. I disagree. I think children (and adults!) must listen and affirm their own self-worth.

I think it's the duty of a parent to help a child understand what makes it special! Assuring the worth of an individual should not arise at the detriment of others. It is important to affirm the ability of a child to develop inner strength, trust and compassion. Before it was common, Mr. Rogers taught self-compassion.

This also instantly led me to think of the 4 S safe connection of Dr Dan Siegel, which children and teenagers need to feel: Seen, Protected, Soothed and Safe.

The truth is that, if you do not first have it for yourself, it is hard (maybe impossible!) to have love, kindness, and acceptance for others!

"Mutual loving relationships call for compassion and patience, empathy, optimism, pleasure in each other's successes, self-confidence and capacity to give without undue benefit thinking."

How Media Can Strengthen Secure Attachment—or Detract From It

Mr. Rogers' Quarter first aired in 1968 at a time when many other shows were searching for entertainment at another cost of character. The documentary mentions cartoon characters who crash into stuff or watch children fall on Nickelodeon.

Rogers saw a need for something entirely different: a display that brought compassion and kindness. Many years later, after 9 September 2011, Mr. Rogers made a public service announcement another way to unify us using broadcast media to ask people to respect each other and to love one another.

Technology can also divide us, while TV and technology can bring us together. Members of the family who sit at the dinner table and fix their eyes to their cell phones cannot give each other a healthy connection.

Won't you be my neighbor? It's a feel-good movie. However, it reminds us that media can bind or break us. It is important to be aware of how we use technology and media. Ask: Is it closer to us, or distant?

"The best thing we can do for each other in times of stress is to listen to each other with one's ears and hearts and be confident that our questions are just as important as our responses."

HOW TO DECODE RELATIONSHIP BEHAVIORS

Relationships can be an integral part of our life, but they can be difficult to manage and challenging experiences. We tend to fall out of love as easily as we fall into it, and we can rebound from relation to relation, or deal with hotness after hotness, to try to find the "one." If we want to create better relationships, we need to be happy, but that means to realize who we are and where we come from.

Our relationships are generally dived by a variety of negative habits that come from our partners as well as ourselves. Whether or not we are involved in this conduct, it can kill our sense of self and lead to a rift between our partners and ourselves when we are reckless. To resolve these habits, we have to ignore them, but still forget them. If you embrace stuff as it is, you can plan to change it. However, that needs you to commit to the journey and all the ups and downs.

RELATIONSHIPS ARE COMPLICATED.

We all have our own ideas about the "dream couple," but many of us fail to achieve the ideal. We fight from relationship to relationship, never find the right one and never feel at ease in the direction we take. Happiness appears to allude to us, and hardships seem to be the rule. We seldom stop struggling through the blind to wonder, "What am I doing wrong? There are a variety of subtle toxic behaviors in our relationships which we indulge in this toxin.

Whether it is emotional manipulation or outright deception, we are pushing our partners away through unaddressed errors, cowardly actions, and fear. We are responsible for the things we do on our own. It's one thing to imagine a successful relationship, but it's another thing to do to create a partnership.

In reality, the development of a relationship with another person requires us to build a better understanding of ourselves and a better understanding of our own limitations and weaknesses. We have to accept who we are and decide what we want ... all that is needed to establish a secure and healthy relationship. Read on to learn why you detonate your relationships or compromise your satisfaction with toxic relationships.

WHY WE DESTROY OUR RELATIONSHIPS.

We don't generally just wake up one day and plan to destroy our relationships. This is a mechanism that develops over time and as a result of bad decisions or wrongdoing. From self-esteem shortcomings to poor perceptions about happiness, these are the key reasons why we kill our joy and relationships.

SELF-ESTEEM DEFICIENCIES

Is self-esteem low? Do you not think you deserve a stable connection or sincere love and affection? The longer you hang on to such values (although you don't know them), the harmer they become in your relationships and your overall outlook on life and romance. You cannot be a trustworthy partner without being a trustworthy person. To feel comfortable interacting with other people, we first have to feel comfortable with who we really are.

HARD-LEARNED LESSONS

The lessons we learn in infancy are life-long experiences. The way we learn to relate and love our parents always goes the same way we relate and love later in life with our partners. While these lessons can provide some shining examples of how to be and love, they may also be destructive lessons that teach us incorrect (or false) "realities" that confuse us and cause us long-term heartache. Though we can experience trauma, it is up to us to eliminate the mess and find a way to appreciate the true nature of our love and compassion.

ALL-OUT COWARDICE

We do not like to say it, but some of us sabotage our ties because we are too afraid to break our friendship. The thought of initiating a breakup can be daunting for those who avoid confrontation at any cost. Does the other partner drag the relationship apart or split it otherwise? This is a passive-aggressive manipulation that seems more at home for the guy who is too afraid to let his partner know he is not in love anymore.

WRONG IDEAS ON HAPPINESS

How do you describe your joy? Does your satisfaction rely on the work you have or the material things you buy? Or is it hindered by whether or not you're romantically partnered? We can describe our happiness in a million different ways, but when that concept does not fit with our true beliefs — we still chase the next best thing. If we have illusions about what happiness is for us, it results in detonations and conflicts in our relationships that could have been prevented with a little self-realization.

THE MOST COMMON WAYS WE DESTROY OUR ROMANTIC RELATIONSHIPS.

From the creation of "me versus you," to mental manipulation — we are addicted to a variety of poisonous behaviors that can cause our romantic relationships. We can't decide how these habits influence people around us. All we can do is take it for what it is and build a strategy to improve it.

Me vs you mentality

Our communication and our ability to work together and to compromise are focused on relationships. It not only makes it impossible for us, as we embrace the mindset 'me vs you,' to resolve conflict, but it also generates the impression that the partner is simply an opponent against which to fight and attack. We must work together to solve challenges, and that is something we can't do if we place goals on one another 's back.

Constant judgement

Under the oppressive weight of relentless judgment, our relationships cannot flourish. Judging our partners will push them further away from us and drive them with their insecurities into risky corners. When we criticize anyone else, we just show our own shortcomings and make it harder for us to be open and honest to those we love.

Secrets and lies

Never will a stable relationship build secrets and lies. When we lie to our friends, we lie to ourselves; and build severe breaches of confidence which can take (if at all) weeks, months and years to resolve. Apart from traditional physical and emotional manipulation, your partner will tell you what you want and your relationship, how you feel, or even what's happening at work or in your social groups. It's all wrong

One-sided perspective

It is toxic to retain a one-sided view in your relationship, and it puts you and your other half seriously together. This happens when you control the relationship or demand that you see it from your viewpoint. There is no compromise in these relationships; you're always right, and always wrong.

Criticizing everything

There is a major difference between giving constructive advice and criticism. Criticality is unwanted, and whatever else that the individual might have done well is not remembered. Whether or not you're a fan of the free sandwich — there's a lot to say about the better, when you inspire someone to change their life in another region.

Emotional manipulation

Too many of us are involved in emotional exploitation, and some of us don't even know what we do. When you manipulate others mentally, you use feelings like depression and anxiety, rather than hitting them to get results. If you sob every time your partner raises doubt, use confidential details, or lift your voice to a hint — you are emotionally exploited (and possibly abused).

Holding the relationship hostage

Will your partner still threaten to break up something that goes wrong for you? If you get angry, do they tell you to go or to tell you that someone like you can't date? The relationship is known as the restoration of the relationship, and it is one of the most highly destructive ways in which we indulge in habits that lead our relationships to the ground.

Confidence betrayals

The trust of our partners and spouses can occur at a variety of levels. In addition to breaking sexual engagement vows, we can trait our partners by sharing them unnecessarily with our friends or even by going back to the home. If you open your partner up to someone in a way that embarrasses or otherwise "outs" you rather keep silent ... you stab them back and take everything that they have right to share (or not).

Zero follow-through

Our love calls for action, and through this action, we show our commitment to our relationships. Words are not enough to keep relationships safe and secure. We must follow through and act behind our declarations of love. If your partner never keeps his promises, it induces disappointment and even anger and resentment.

Beating-them into a corner

Beating your partner in the corner is never all right — even though you do it figuratively. Going for what you want, or for the compromise you want, is one thing, but chasing your partner for something or talking about what you want to talk about is another. Partnerships all include sharing and taking, and that means finding consensus and learning how to do things on the terms of others as well as ours (and respecting their limits as we do).

No vulnerability

Is your partner not vulnerable? Fear of lowering your walls or letting them see who you really are inside? This is a natural fear but also prevents us from touching the deepest aspects of love and connection. To build a relationship that will stand the test of time, you must know one another intimately and trust one another. This is something that is open and knows how to let others in.

Unable to stepup to the plate

We are all responsible for our own path on this planet, and for the things we do right and the things we get wrong, we are all accountable. You are driving your partner away when you cannot apologize or take responsibility for the mistakes you have made – or if you blame someone else for your problems or the problems you are facing in your relationship (though you do not know this). You push them to hate you, and they're always going to see the facts.

Sense of entitlement

In a partnership, there is nothing worse than a partner with a true sense of right. It's perfectly appropriate to feel like you have the right to work for something, but it's completely unfair to feel like someone just owes you to something. Just because you live in a relationship does not mean that you have the right to the company, ideas or resources of your partner automatically. Such actions come from a place of reverence and honor.

BEHAVIORS THAT SIGNAL A RELATIONSHIP IS IN TROUBLE

While there are endless explanations why truthful partnerships don't, some very strong signs are there that partners should be aware of this. These destructive acts can take many forms, but they can all undermine the fundamental faith and close relationships that have been successful.

All intimate partners, whether they are newly in love or engaged spouses, need to be watchful if one of them is behaving in any of the following eight ways.

1. The Distribution of Resources Change

Intimate relationship tools include money, time, affection, availability and interest. How each partner shares these resources is an example of how equal and important each other feels.

When love is fresh, the resources which feed the relationship are freely shared and freely shared. Unfortunately, when love loses its initial illusion and luster, the spouses are often more self-serving and have rights to these tools.

You will begin to complain more that you don't get what you think you should and that the improvements are of little benefit or concern to each other.

These are the kind of declarations which are obvious warning signs:

"When I need you, you're never around anymore."

"You're spending more time with your friends now than with me."

"You're a lot longer at work. Have you an affair? "Why are you so much texting?

"Together, we used to do so many things. Now, you're tired all the time.

But if you get other things you're more interested in, you have the ability to do them unexpectedly. "Why do you waste so much money that has nothing to do with us? "We still used to cuddle before work in the morning.

Before I can even wake up, you're out of here. These types of comments represent the priority changes that the partners once had for each other.

They demonstrate that other desires use resources which were once reserved for the relationship.

2. A Partner Seems Preoccupied

Remember if you were not able to wait to speak to your partner? When you were reconnected, the first thing you would do was to concentrate on each other and catch up on how long you were apart. You were also a top priority for each other and ready to reunite before the other demands of life interfered.

Link bids, availability, enforcement, inquiry and love appear to be deaf ears. Either or both partners are concerned about something more significant at the moment than being completely present.

It may sound like one, or both partners are storing, dreaming, focusing on something more important or just not interested in what the other says or needs. The other partner starts to feel ignored, forgotten or not significant.

These are the forms of words that are strong signs of warning:

"I'm going to go out of the shower completely naked, and you still don't look up."

"If I ask you about the job, you give me summaries or brief answers like you're not involved in what's happening there. You used to ask me about your choices and needed my advice.

"I asked you three times, and you don't even look up, or you simply tell me to find out where you want to go to dinner. We used to think that putting these things together was fun.

"I shouldn't say what I need to you. You used to know. You used to know. Now, when I know that you already have the stuff, you want me to give you a manual.

"We're neither cuddling nor chatting in bed. You either read or peer into the ceiling. Do I no longer matter to you? Tell me what's going on, please.

"Hi? Hi? Is there anyone in there? "What is happening, sweetheart.

You seem so nervous and sound like you are shutting me out.

3. A PARTNER QUICKLY SHUTS DOWN COMMUNICATION

If love is fresh, most couples have a profound interest in the thoughts, feelings and needs of each other. Concentration, composure and persistence are met with attempts at communication. Curiosity and persistent curiosity meet any new concept.

As intimate partners lose interest or become too capable of predicting answers and explanations, they often use responses that restrict the effort to prolong the interaction. Capping is a strategy, conscious or unconscious, that prevents the other partner from making an effort to communicate effectively.

Imagine any of these answers to your scope to share with your partner. Would you like to continue to express what you thought or felt?

"That's a dumb idea."

"You still complain about the actions of your mother. What are you doing to get her to behave in this way? "Out of a molehill, you make a mountain."

"Why do you let these things bother you like this.

Just let them go. Just let them go. "I heard you lament over and over about this stuff.

Make real what to expect. "You've done WHAT?

"This discussion is completely boring." "Here, I believe you are far too reactive.

Give a break to the other guy.

"Let me tell you how you ought to have done this." "If you'd just learn to listen, people would be opening up more to you."

4. PARTNERS BECOME MORE NEGATIVELY REACTIVE

Passion and enthusiasm are excellent qualities which usually improve a partnership. They derive from the passion, desire and engagement of a person in the things that make him or her alive and excited.

Yet they share an emotional relationship with a dark twin. As intensity levels are associated with negative reactivity, the partner will possibly be squeezed and defeated on the other end.

Negative reactivity is a sequence of actions that turn on the receiver curtly and despicably. They display irritability, impatience, denial and are burdened with the offer to communicate. Whether the snapping partners are concerned about personal issues or something they don't like about their other spouses, they send a clear message that they don't want the interaction.

Many who connect well with each other know each other when they are inaccessible and share when they are more accessible. They would also like to know the value of the needs of their partner at the moment and take that into account.

It is up to the other partner without that integrity to find out if it is okay to communicate or to risk the curt and reckless answer.

There are common remarks that should be taken into account as warning signs:

"Why always choose the wrong time to chat with me? "I just can't understand your nonsense."

"What makes you believe that when it's convenient for you, you will bother me?

"Come and talk to me if you have to say anything important." "You know that when I'm in the middle of something, I don't want to talk."

"You are so profoundly vulnerable.

Can't you talk about this for a change to someone else?

"With your relentless demands, you are wearing out your welcome. Right now, I told you I don't want to talk about it.

5. A PARTNER IS SECRETIVE

Transparency, sincerity and integrity are key behaviors that I have seen in any good relationship. They are features of open communication, which allows pairs profoundly to know each other, what to expect and how to manage it.

Secrecy is the opposite of such behavior. It is intended to retain information from a partner so that choices are avoided if he or she knows. It varies significantly from the privacy to which everyone has a right. Privacy does not harm the confidence of a partnership. It is just the right to retain thoughts and feelings towards oneself that must be addressed from within the individual and not potentially dangerous to the other party.

When intimate partners keep secrets, they act in ways that contrast with what they think they believe or do. When asked, they are usually defensive, evasive or answers questions in an unreasonable or nonsensical manner, which makes the other partners more uncomfortable and unable to understand the difference between what they see and what they hear.

Passive/aggressive behavior may sometimes have the same effect. A passive/aggressive partner promises more than he or she can offer and, if such commitment is not kept, prevents any conflict. Sadly, all habits, which appear or sound hidden, usually scare partners at the other end. Their begging questions, never addressed in full transparency, only serve to increase their vulnerability.

The partners feel that these words are often omitted from the truth:

"Are you coming home from the office later and later at night? Is there something going on? "We were lying in bed in the morning, chatting in the morning.

You're up now, showered out before I woke up even? Where are you going? Where are you going? "Are you going out again for dinner with your girlfriends? You didn't come home until eleven last week, and you were great.

Has someone else taken you home? "Several cash withdrawals from our bank account last month. For what have you used them? "Your best friend called you to come here last night.

You told me that you were out with him for dinner. Where have you been?

"Somebody in the middle of the night tells you? You take it away from me when I hit your phone and tell me that this is a nuisance call. This week three times? Yeah, that's good.

Who is it? Who is it? "You have changed your iPad password without telling me. That never happened before. That never happened before. Are you hiding something?

6. THE RELATIONSHIP FEELS STAGNANT

Discovery is the key contributor in every romantic relationship I overcome predictability and boredom to continued enthusiasm, curiosity and desire. The constant influx of new knowledge keeps both partners engaged and involved in new relationships.

So many times, the partners in active relationships learn more about each other and avoid finding or creating new adventures. As if you once ran a great race together and have now become the pit-stops where you literally fuel and send out the most thrilling bits of yourself.

Often couples question the boredom of dull predictability by searching together for new experiences outside the partnership. Alternatively, one or both may have interests beyond the partnership and share these findings.

When several partners start to feel bored, or partnership, they normally ask for more interesting things together first. If those requests are overlooked or delayed, they generally try harder to stimulate or locate others for a while. If the supplications are still ignored, the relationship may stagnate, and the partner who is bored will pursue life elsewhere.

The following are examples of how to get more excited:

"Honey, we never really do something nice."

"These days, you seem so into yourself. You hardly like you used to share your life with me. What's happening to you? "In our sex life, we seem so predictable and mechanical.

Do you feel the same? Will you like anything else? "I've asked you so much not to speak the same thing every time we go to dinner. We must stimulate each other more, don't you think?

"Can we take some time aside and schedule a real holiday, just the two of us? We're in a rut, and I'm very concerned. "I hate to say this, sweetie, but with our relationship, I'm really bored.

I don't blame any of us, but I just need to look forward to something else. The same old one, the same old, really doesn't cut it for me anymore.

"You know when we're out with other friends; you're the party star. Nobody would want to date the guy with whom I live.

7. MORE FIGHTING

One of the foundations of a strong partnership is an effective dispute resolution. Partners who are able to perceive differences and issues without bias or expectation and who actively discuss them benefit from their disagreements.

Couples that do get into problems like anyone else, but do not repeatedly echo the same points. So, they debrief when they are both settled down. Like a great football team or business team, they chat about their own obligations, find out the next time they can do better, and reassure each other that they will do their utmost to uphold these agreements.

When disputes are not resolved successfully, they lead to anger, martyrdom or withdrawal and continue to develop. Whenever the same problem reoccurs, these negative relationships evolve over time. Relationships strengthen as the percentage of unproductive claims decrease and worsen as they increase.

Sounds like this as the negative experiences become more prominent:

"My effort to resolve something with you is disgusting. We're all going through the same sick reasons, and it never gets better.

"You're going to play the game again, so I'm going to end up being the bad guy again? Why don't you just drop this act and tell me that you don't like me, all right? "You behave like you try to get me to take the whole blame.

We both know that you want to end the debate and you think I will go away if you agree with me. Okay, guess what, guess what? This time, that's not going to happen. "We didn't have the same go-around 100 times.

We both know that when you can't get your way out of the house. Why don't you just do it now and get it over? "I don't even know why I'm trying to speak with you. You never listen, and you think you're still right.

"Don't just walk in and begin belly harvesting. When you don't even ask what happens first, I'm sick of your constant complaining?

8. YOU'VE STOPPED TOUCHING AS MUCH

Not everyone needs the same amount of physical contact, whether in love, sexual intimacy or just being close to each other. Over time, most couples find a balance between their desires and strive to define differences.

When these relationships alter markedly over time, the spouse who experiences this shift may show his or her frustration more likely. The other person will justify these legitimate reasons if he or she cares about stress, illness or a tragedy and the couple can do so until the normal physical relationship has been restored. But if this change reflects a gradual one-way pull-off, the partnership may be challenging.

These are the usual signs of a missing person:

"Honey, what's the matter. Whenever I hit you, you pull away. You're upset with me? "Tell me, please, if you're no longer drawn to me.

It's very difficult to see you transform into bed without the hugs we had. "You seem to give me a smooth, quick one when I ask for a hug.

Am I demanding too much? "You have some difficulties getting excited. Do you have a concern in which you need to tell me?

"Hey." Hey. Who's in the picture if you're not interested in me? "I'm beginning to feel like there's something wrong about you.

I don't seem to strike, but you don't. Please just tell me if you're too far away for a reason? "Okay, honey.

Sex on the weekends and, now? What the fuck is happening?

HOW TO SHARPEN YOUR RELATIONSHIP SKILLS

Enhancing skills can have many advantages. They help to sustain relationships and can advance your career. Emotional intelligence and self-awareness can enhance communication and increase trust. Various techniques can help you develop people's skills in tough circumstances or just in daily life.

DEVELOP EMOTIONAL INTELLIGENCE

Emotional intelligence enables people to be conscious and responsible for emotions. Strengthening emotional intelligence can help people control their emotions. Emotional intelligence growth includes:

- • Learn how to respond with knowledge and interpersonal skills

- • Hold feelings under control

- • Understand other people's tension and anxiety to control their own emotions properly

- • Settlement of disputes

In any partnership, a certain amount of tension is inevitable. The following are several ways to create conflict resilience:

FOCUS ON THE PRESENT

Respect others without manipulating their feelings or outcomes

Emphasis instead of winning or losing a contract on compromise

LISTENING SKILLS

When you learn to listen, people will pay more attention to your needs. You can not only learn more of what is happening in other people's lives but also feel more connected to them. Including:

- • Note voice tone and non-verbal signals

- • Listening before answering

- • Passive listening to encourage another individual to talk

RESPECT DIFFERENCES

Recitation for and understanding of cultural differences in life. We learn much of the skills of parents and members of the community. It helps to be mindful of cultural differences when interacting with someone from a different culture. Respectful communication requires eye touches, work with laughter and lightheartedness despite misunderstandings, and aim to encourage greater understanding.

MAINTAIN RELATIONSHIPS

When mutual respect is given, it is easier to sustain a partnership. Relationships do not build on a weak surface connection; they may take months or even years to develop a stable relationship with an individual based on deepening confidence and mutual understanding. It takes a lot of time, but the challenge is worth finding the first connections that are mutually beneficial and supportive when things are challenging and when they go well. Human beings are made for attachment so that learning how to sustain them will make you feel powerful and safe.

HOW TO USE EFFECTIVE COUPLE COMMUNICATION

The secret to any effective relationship is good communication since relationships are emotional and rely on verbal and nonverbal interpersonal interactions between the two persons involved. Most marriages begin with the assumption that the first cause of divorce is miscommunication. Communication is even more important in cases of parenting and co-parenting when parents raise adult children. Children learn from their parents or guardians their first communication techniques. Three kinds of communication are available: verbal, nonverbal and written. Below are the top 10 effective pair of communication techniques. This list was taken from meta-research performed on several internet lists, books, interviews and the past experience of this blogger.

1. DO NOT TALK AT THE SAME TIME – LISTEN!

This may seem straightforward, but when tensions increase, everyone wishes to get their point across, and a subliminal power struggle comes into play, which means no one really cares about the discussion or resolution. Do not disturb each other, please. Continuous interference shows you that the other person has nothing to say and that you only want your way. The reason for the discussion is to listen to one another's views. Stop the temptation to crack.

2. THINK BEFORE YOU SPEAK OR YOU WILL REGRET IT

"Give me a hearing gift." – King Solomon said. You can claim something you can't ever take back. If you can't talk in person, try writing, but stay away from the internet. You express one another's personal feelings. Send in short phrases to each other. Write a note or text. However, contact in real-time is better. Please NO CAPS. Form in all the caps gives the feeling that you scream. I LOVE YOU are allowed. You love each other, remember. Remember.

3. GIVE A HOOT – CARE

It is so important not to lose sight when communicating with your spouse or partner that contact is important to ensure that the connection is not broken. Place yourself in the shoes of the other person. Try to understand why you feel the way you do. Have they all the facts? Do they really want you to pay attention? Nevertheless, treat your feelings as significant.

For example, if your partner shows disappointment that you are not invited to a significant social event. You think the whole thing is dumb, on the other hand. Do not express your thoughts and feel comfortable with your partner. "I know that was important to you, but let's try to find out why we weren't invited so that we can be invited to another event or the same one." These are the little things that count.

4. NO HITTING BELOW THE BELT

Watch your language, please. One of the things that can interrupt successful contact is to call or lift something that happened a long time ago. In specific, a circumstance which has been resolved or forgiven. Please try to avoid the words "you" and "you always," which would definitely lead you to a negative discussion. Try to mark your partner's first name instead lovingly. This strategy is diluting wrath. It shifts the conversation's tone.

5. FACTS, PLEASE

One rule for married couples a long time is, you can inquire about it, but you have to let it go if you can't prove it. In other words, don't bring it to the table if there is no proof. Suspicion is one thing, but it's another matter to accuse others of it. Many partners are tired of being accused of fraud. Many cheaters say they have been accused of always cheating, so they really chose to do it. It's normal to be a little jealous about the love of your life, but when you feel it, it is not natural to show it. A discreet investigation is allowed, but allegations are not allowed without certainty.

6. PARTICIPATE WITH SINCERITY AND HONESTY

Two people chat. Two people talk. Silent therapy is not required. Hate is not the opposite of passion but indifference. Talkback without any hidden agendas when your partner talks to you. Communicate with integrity and accountability. Send explanation questions. If you're busy, ask for a time when both of you can find things better. Don't just go out or listen and don't talk. Know that you are together in this relationship.

7. OBSERVATION

One way of connecting is to hear what your partner doesn't say. Two people in a relationship learn fears, aspirations, beliefs and desires from each other. Therefore, nobody can know your partner better than you, use this for your benefit and observe the situation. Some people articulate themselves better or communicate better than others. For instance, Rita knew that her husband, an advertising manager, wanted a new look. He got a couple of pounds, so she thought he was aware of it. She thought he wanted to be more appealing to her, but after seeing his online search for clothing, she realized he needed a new search because his style was dating and he was placed at a competitive disadvantage while he worked with his younger colleagues. It wasn't about their friendship. Rita hired a professional stylist to solve the dilemma of her husband.

8. BODY LANGUAGE IS A NON-VERBAL COMMUNICATION TECHNIQUE

While the language of the body is something to study, it talks clearly. When your wife speaks, seeing him or her in the eyes means your wife has your indivisible attention. To lean forward means that you are interested in what they say, catching the eye is a sign of dishonesty. Learn the body language of your partner. Michael heard, for example, that Amber had numerous walks for her moods. There was a walk when she was tired, one was angry and a completely different walk when she was comfortable. Michael is also tuned in the language of her body to sense her mood and to spend some time with her. Do not disregard their body language when engaging with your partner because this is how you will decide whether they understand, agree or disagree.

9. RESPECT – AGREE TO DISAGREE

Don't lose sight of the two on the same team, and there's no need to weaken or to battle each other because there will always be another problem along the way. Couples who learn together to solve problems are the most popular. Every issue cannot be overcome because from time to time, you and your partner are people who have different views. Be mindful that the relationship is greater than any issue. In addition, value your partner by being a trustee on whom you can rely. Ten-year-old Sherry and her husband Mike never agree on political candidates. It was much like sports, and for the rival teams, they were cheering. However, they were still on the same side at the end of an election, regardless of political problems.

10. WITNESSES OR **THIRD-PARTY** INTERVENTION

Many couples are looking for therapy, a trusted friend or a family member to play a neutral party. This is not a myth. A third party may take a different view of the situation. Be sure the person is a trustworthy individual and has the expertise to help you with the problem. Janet wanted her husband, for example, to be a little less conventional. His views about the role of women in marriage were very old-fashioned. He never washed or housework a dish. Janet worked. Janet worked. She and Bob had a new sweetheart. Janet felt that she needed Bob's further support. He did not agree. He did not agree. Janet went to Bob's dad for support. He spoke to Bob and expressed his own experiences of changing his views on a man's place in the family. Then Bob decided to help out.

Finally, good communication is one of the best qualities that couples should acquire to strengthen their partnership and marriage.

Communicate Tips for Couples and Everyone Else.

Relations with mothers, husbands, daughters, boyfriends or even friends are some of the biggest challenges of life. While a variety of factors contribute to the success of a marriage or a long-term relationship, communication skills – or absence of them – can improve or impede one 's prospects.

Would you like to change how you interact with your important another person?

General Communication Tips

1.) Active Listening / Use Feedback:

Often, when we listen to our other important person (or someone else), we're not fully present. We might be distracted by something important in our life or feel overly reactive to their intense emotions. During occasional talk (and particularly during heated conversations), it is common for people to be impatiently waiting to chuckle in with a thought (defensive argument, refutations etc.) while the other talks, instead of just getting all in and then answering later. Therefore, we don't pay complete attention to what the other thinks.

In the other hand, "good listening" means working together to slow down and to listen with an open heart and mind. That's better said than done, of course! But the purpose is crucial, so you have to start there. If you don't listen closely and honestly for some reason, then you might want to table talk, debate, etc. for another time (again, more easily informed than done).

You will continue to listen actively by providing feedback. The classical way to do this is to reaffirm what the other person has learned, to prove your comprehension. It feels amazing to be heard;we all know. Being seen and heard is calming and cannot alter the environment in a constructive manner significantly. You don't really have to agree with what is said, but you want to prove that you get the best viewpoint from the other. It's okay to be absolutely clear. You might say, for example, "It sounds as though you are angry at me for forgiving, or I understand you correctly? Like so many facets of communication, active listening is a skill and often takes practice.

When we do it more, we strengthen it, and it becomes simpler.

2.) Edit Criticism:

Make a deliberate effort to avoid personal criticism when engaging with your partner. This involves avoiding putdowns, threats, and offensive body language, including eye-rolling. Criticism, as we all know, makes people feel defensive; this greatly hampers the empathy process and can contribute to a further increase of feelings of frustration and injury.

3.) Be Gentle:

When you are depressed, bring it up quietly and without blame. Know the sound used to address issues. A tone of mutual respect – one which is either passive or hostile – is very critical in initiating a constructive conversation.

4.) Seek First to Understand vs Being Understood:

This is one of my favorite strategies and can always be used as a mantra in all conversations, with partners, other family members or friends. When in confrontation, our emotional response is always based on our need to be understood. So much did you hear, "You don't understand what I mean! "Of course, healthy partnerships require mutual understanding, but instead of stressing your own need to be understood, strive to shift the emphasis and concentrate on understanding others. This can also change the nature of connection and pave the way for transparent and fresh contact.

5.) Ask Open-Ended Questions:

Hmm, did you note the rhetorical questions like "You still stop talking and listening? "Or" I wonder if without asking me you would ever pick up the trash? "Audio dialogue doesn't seem to start? Yeah, they might sound good to say right now, as you release some frustration or rage. But it does not lead to compromises in the long run.

Rather, ask questions open-ended if you have issues. For example, you can tell your wife, "I can use more support to clean the garbage. Do you have any ideas on how we can do this?

6.) Stay Calm:

Try to keep negotiations as smooth as possible. If things start to escalate, take a break and meet again when you both have a less emotional feeling. Keep yourself in mind; do you tell yourself anything which keeps you reasonably calm or fuel the flames of emotional distress?

7.) Use "I" statements:

Try to control your emotions by using "I" phrases (e.g. I feel, I need to, I want to). Remember the strategy "XYZ": "I feel X in situations Z when you do Y." For instance, "I'm annoyed when you don't clean the trash on Thursday, the day you agree."

8.) Self-soothing:

Seeking ways to calm down when you get angry. For starters, take a "time out," take a walk or a while to do some breathing exercises. These concerns areholding feelings under balance. Talks would be even more effective if feelings are more controlled.

9.) Accept Influence from the Other:

Try to put yourself in the shoes of your partner and take their opinions and ideas with you. The research done by Dr John Gottman shows that "marriage works in such a way as to ensure that the husband can have control from his wife." Therefore, be aware of the dynamics that can promote or hinder the ability to influence one another in your connection.

10.) Share Appreciations:

Every person will feel loved and appreciated for who they are in any successful relationship. It can be helpful to consider what you admire in someone and say certain things while talking. Research by Gottman shows that effective people make five times as many positive comments as negative ones in solving issues.

Sharing gratitude leads to a number of positive emotions, and when they feel good, people actually think and interact better.

STRATEGIES FOR ENDING ARGUMENTS

Research by Dr John Gottman suggests that relationship success does not depend on whether or not couples argue. That's how they think about it. Conflicts are inevitable in any romantic relationship and can lead to development if managed with an eye instead of growing stress.

Here are a few examples of ways to deal productively with claims. As with any approach, it is important to be aware that one is best for a particular situation, which is often easier said than done.

1.) Validate and Apologize:

Let your partner know that by validating them, you respect their point of view. It can sound simple, but do not forget to take responsibility for what you did and, if possible, apologize.

2.) Change the topic of conversation in a gentle, sensitive manner:

Change the subject of conversation if you have a point that doesn't go anywhere. In a gentle and attentive way, it is crucial that the other person does not feel neglected. This strategy would fit well for certain claims. But with highly charged subjects, a follow-up time might be required to discuss what is relevant for both participants.

3.) Use humor:

If used at the right time, levity will go a long way. If you are caught in a loop of misery, try to make it better with some laughter or ignorance. Often a few will snap out of a trance of rage. Like other techniques, it is crucial that you know how and when to use humor in order to avoid trivializing your significant others.

4.) Yield to the other:

Let your relationship go by understanding the importance of the viewpoint of your partner. Often, it's appropriate to say so as long as you don't always have to do so to end a conversation. Alternatively, you should "agree to disagree" and move on.

5.) Make physical contact:

In a conflict, partners typically feel very distant, which can fuel the negative cycle. Reach out with supportive physical expressions to your important partner, such as raising your hand or placing your arm around your shoulders. This can shift the nature of relation rapidly to one that is more caring and less adversarial by growing the sense of connection and security. Since contact can trigger border breaches, it can be a good idea to ask before you take this measure.

6.) Take a break and re-approach later:

It's like rebooting your machine hard. Enable things to shut down for a while and start again later. This can pave the way for a new viewpoint, which is lacking in unproductive, redundant claims.

7.) Acknowledge common ground between the two of you:

As they disagree, people tend to focus on their beliefs and become more divided as things worsen. Although, in most of the cases, all sides find common ground. Find this middle ground and speak clearly about it.

8.) Set a timer:

If you are trapped in an argument, each person talks and doesn't listen very well to each other, agree to set a timer. Offer one person 5 minutes of time, for example, to say all that is in mind while the other person listens without interruption. When the time passes, turn to another person and give him 5 minutes of undivided attention. Many people just want to feel validated and noticed. By agreeing to set a timer, every party can express its concern and feel control over the process, which tends to lessen the burden of emotions.

Principles for dealing with conflict

We all live and work with people, but everyone is different. And it's even more difficult if you are a businessman, the boss. You don't just work with people; you also work with people who work with people who work with people. As a leader, you are responsible for the outcomes and still have to get people to succeed and work together. Human relations are inevitably complex and contradictory.

All good leaders will finally learn some crucial lessons from dispute resolution. There aren't many of them – only around eight. But if you do not know these eight essential concepts and apply them, human problems will make your leadership chaotic, and your life is exhausting. It is, therefore, necessary to learn the eight principles – three criteria and five steps.

The eight fundamental principles of highly effective conflict resolution.

"A leader must have a strategy in his or her organization for coping with conflict. Leaders must overcome conflicts at source by improving relationships and better knowing the desires on both sides of the dispute.

ADOPT THE RIGHT MINDSET

When they face confrontation, most people do a lot of wrong things. For example, they typically avoid conflicts at almost every cost and often take care of their hurts for a long time before they talk to another, often talk about a conflict with other people instead of the one who can truly solve the problem and sometimes chat or criticize them for trying to feel better about themselves and the situation.

When they attempt to converse with the other person in dispute, often people want to take the easy route by leaving a message online, by mailing a speech, or by sending a letter. In reality, these forms of avoidance cause more problems.

All these errors, and others like them, are the product of the confusion, and small problems or misunderstandings can lead to serious problems.

Top leaders prevent such failures when they take the correct view.

precondition 1
Address the responsible party explicitly and promptly instead of damage.

Speak to the person who hurt you if you've been hurt by others. Explicitly. Explicitly. Don't wait. Don't wait. Do it immediately.

Orrin Woodward discussed this important subject in his speech entitled "Conflict Resolution – Relationships for Life:

"Controversy is like a fire. Simple to snuff out if it is small but almost unmanageable if it is not treated easily. Imagine going to bed at night and looking at your bedroom corner and seeing a tiny flame splashing out. You prefer to forget it and go to bed knowing that in the morning you'll talk to it. If you like your home, this is probably not a good idea. And it's not a reasonable plan to address the issue directly and immediately if you want to maintain good relations and progress.

Often, it's complicated, but it can be summarized as follows how genuine leaders react to conflict or even possible conflicts:

- • Explain can requirements have not been fulfilled.

- • Brainstorm and give the other person the best intentions.

- • Explicitly approach the other person and speak to him or her.

- • Using the following five measures

- • Do all of this directly, without any harm or resentment.

This is the first and necessary precondition: deal with disputes immediately by direct communication with other parties.

precondition 2
Speak to the other side rather than gossip.

All too many people who feel hurt stop talking directly to the other person. Instead, they speak to a lot of other people. This is gossip. This is gossip. This is critique, too. And they are both the enemies of leadership and achievement.

Conflicts will take place, people will be, and there will be misunderstandings, hurts and broken expectations and other disputes. Members are aware of this and are planning for it. In particular, if hurt or disagreement happens, they take action by:

- • Explain what standards have not been met.

- • Giving the other person the best intentions

- • Do not cause fears, accidents or other adverse effects to become greater

- • Never laugh or mock the other side.

- • Approach another person to fix problems directly and with love (using five steps)

- • Do all this straight away without allowing negative feelings time to develop.

- • This is the path to leadership, the responsible way to respond to conflict.

precondition 3
Confront disputes rather than rely on electronic communications

Even when people take the correct perspective, they make the mistake of implicitly expressing disagreements and negative events. This is typically done via e-mail, voice or social media.

The problem is that any non-interactive contact appears to intensify – not clean – the fire of conflict.

Whenever you have something unpleasant to share, particularly when dealing with a dispute, do so face-to-face, if possible, and at least in person on the phone (or using one of the many today's video chat options). Never use non-interactive formats to try to settle the dispute. If you have to send an email or leave a message, simply be optimistic and let the person know you'd love to speak to them and welcome their call. Then communicate with them directly in person.

The greater the negative, hurt or disagreement actual or future, the more you have to be to work together for a better solution. Do it in person if the dispute is intense or strongly emotional. Never attempt to settle the dispute by text, social media or voice mail.

THE 5 STEPS OF EFFECTIVE CONFLICT RESOLUTION.

Now, when we take the right perspective, it's time to speak about five phases. Take action if there is a disagreement between you, or anyone else.

Step 1 – Affirm the relationship

The measures of highly successful conflict resolution are clear and straightforward with the correct attitude. Step 1 is friendship validation. Sit back and say to the other party: "I might be uncomfortable, but I'm here because I respect our friendship much more than my comfort and information."

Tell me, "I'm sure there was a mistake, and I want to know how I should have done better, and then get it right."

Do this in a spirit of compassion, affection and genuine determination to transcend any differences. This is the first step.

At the outset of any dispute resolution, it is critically necessary to do this. Possibly the entire resolution will collapse if you try to skip this stage. It's so necessary and strong.

Step 2 – Genuinely seek for understanding

If you validate the relationship to the extent where other people feel more complete on their emotional bank account and are able to get to work, the next step is to look for understanding. Don't begin by making sure the other party understands you; first, concentrate on the other party understanding.

What were the expectations not fulfilled for her? What happened to this misunderstanding? What happened? (Often what you think was happening and what was actually happening isn't exactly the same.) What was she thinking? What was she thinking? Since what did she think?

There are crucial things to understand and generally explain what has actually happened. This will eliminate several misunderstandings. But with these direct questions, it is necessary not just to annoy the other person. Let her describe them in her own terms, rather than in her own language. Listen carefully. Most people aren't very successful, but leaders need to make it a top skill. Listen, really.

The secret to listening efficiency is the mirror effect, which gives us the technique of mirrors. This means that you represent what the other person says to you. It's quite easy; it's just one point you make. Top leaders know it's a must. Usually, you won't experience any successful dispute resolution if you don't do this.

The look is amazingly strong. It tells the other person that you listen, and it also tells you that you listen. Mirroring keeps you focused on what the other person actually does, and on what you need, want and feel. If you're not voicing words from other people, you're not listening either. Because if you don't listen to the person you don't feel listened to, and you don't fix anything.

People need to be heard, and they should feel understood when they do. Only then will they be mentally able to think about concrete solutions. If you really want to settle a problem, you just have to try to grasp it first. Listen carefully and use Mirror Technique time and again until the other person tells you you heard him entirely.

Step 3 – Lovingly seek to be understood.
The most important term here is loving! If you don't like your answers, you usually fall on deaf ears. How your messages sometimes feel is more important than the actual words you use. When you lovingly share your thoughts and feelings about the situation, note that the resolution is your goal. The aim is to clarify how you didn't feel about what the other party should have done.

Step 3 is necessary even though step 1 and step 2 fix several misunderstandings and hurt feelings. Another person wants good emotions from the fact that he really knew what was happening. Then, talk about the issues – he needs to hear from your viewpoint and share your views about the dispute, so you can avoid letting residual emotions develop and become stronger.

It is very important not to make a regular yet hurtful mistake as the conversation continues. Do not give the other individual reasons or speak in an attack. For instance, say, "You didn't call, and I felt, but don't say," You didn't call intentionally, that made me feel like that.

Both the motivation and blame are accusatory and anger, and the listener is inclined to feel and respond defensively. Share your experience and how it made you feel, not to comment on the feelings, actions or activities of another person.

When both parties have expressed their views and concerns freely, simply and lovingly and both feel respected and understood, there can be a genuine and substantive resolution of a dispute. In fact, both parties may have stronger relationships and connections than before the dispute.

Step 4 – Own the responsibility and sincerely apologize.
"True leaders pursue ways to be transparent while protecting the other party's ego. It takes two to tango and two to fail. None of us is perfect so you can always take some responsibility for it if there is a disagreement. Even if you are not sure that there was a disagreement, you may take the responsibility not to communicate more clearly and to know how someone else feels.

Your words should be genuine and honest, but start taking responsibility when you see anything you can do better. Don't hold those stuff in your mouth, vocalize it freely and say you're sorry. In so doing, you show that you do your best, all you can to solve the situation and restore the full sense of friendship and cooperation. It's strong.

You will be terrible at resolving conflicts, and many people won't want to work with you if you do not take responsibility for everything you could have done better. This is a sure way of reducing your authority and undermining your leadership and progress. When it is time for accountability, in every dispute resolution, we hit a normal turning point. Any chance we fail when we should or could take honest responsibility is a strike against us. This is an integral component of leadership. Without it, there is no leadership, so trust is lost. Leaders take responsibility not only for any errors but also for not intensifying and doing everything they could have done to avoid problems or improve things.

If we want to be better leaders or resolve conflicts, we need real confidence. True confidence is only restored when both parties see and willingly accept responsibility for anything they have done badly or could have done better. If this does not happen, there is no resolution. If you take responsibility, apologize sincerely, do so as often as you can. But always apologize, not away from duty.

Once you have accepted responsibility for and apologized for your involvement in the case, and once the other person did the same, don't let your subconscious remind you of everything the other party did wrong. Go on. Move on. He is excused, and you have forgiven him. Leaders focus on what is actually important, not previously resolved issues. If you want to be a leader, adhere to this norm completely.

Step 5 – Seek agreement

Both sides reiterated the value of the partnership at this stage, both were heard and both excused. Both parties should now strive to improve and reinforce their future relations. This is a vital move because nothing remains in place. Things are changing.

Agree that in future, both of you will avoid making the same errors by always talking to one another quickly and clearly if there is any problem.

Still spend some time dreaming about the future and electricity. As part of every dispute resolution, whether between you and someone else or as a leader to support other people, ask yourself what is the potential in your conflict. Brainstorm ways to seize this chance together. Leaders are not settling a dispute; they are searching for ways to make it a big success together.

"Life is best viewed as an adventure."

If you have finished phase 1-4 and the problem has been solved, note that it is not really solved until you have found the chance. This means getting together and looking for consensus on something that you really need or want to do together.

BLANK WORKSHEETS

What if I told you that there was a magic formula for a relationship? You wouldn't believe me, I'm sure, and with good reason!

How complicated partnerships can be seen easily. If there were a truly successful way of enjoying safe and happy ties, surely someone would have packaged it and sold it right now?

Until we discover the 100% good formula is guaranteed for a perfect relationship, we must do what we have – build our relationship skills, communicate effectively, engage in activities that strengthen our connections and use couple counselling to resolve any major problems.

COUPLES COUNSELING EXERCISES, WORKSHEETS, & TECHNIQUES

If you don't have the time or the energy to read a couple of therapy novel, that's okay. There are simpler and easier ways to learn more about your spouse and strengthen your bond, also helped by couples and therapists.

Below are some of the most popular drills, workbooks and techniques.

1. Soul Gazing
This is an enjoyable exercise that allows you and your partner to interact more deeply. It can have an immense effect on your sense of connection, so it's not for the weak heart!

Face your partner in a seated position to attempt this exercise. Touch each other so closely that the hands almost meet and look into the eyes of each other.

Keep the eye for 3 to 5 minutes. Don't worry; this isn't a game- you should blink! Still, refrain from speaking. Just look into each other's eyes, even if at first it's awkward. If your silence is awkward, choose a song that you like or is important in your relationship and keep your eye contact until the song ends.

And popular culture has gained insight into this exercise's influence.

2. Extended Cuddle Time

This is just as straightforward — and fun — as it sounds! The guidelines are to cuddle more often.

Distraction from a mobile phone, tablet or book is easy when you're sleeping, but cuddling is really a much better way to end your day. When we cuddle with our partner, the chemicals released boost our mood, reinforce our bond, and even help us sleep better.

This exercise is to be done just before bed, but you can carve to cuddle at any time of the day if you do not sleep for yourself. It is necessary to get a moment, to display physical affection and to improve your intimacy with your partner.

Relationship expert Jordan Gray recommends cuddling to a music playlist when you have issues locating or participating in a daily cuddle session. You can get in a bit of cuddling, while watching a movie or when you both wake up in the morning – but it works best for you.

3. The 7 Breath-Forehead Connection Exercise

This exercise is a perfect way to get away from the activities around you and concentrate on your partner.

Either lie down with your partner on your side or sit upright with your partner. Face each other and kindly align the brows. Make sure your chins are turned down so that you don't rub nose and linger for a few breaths.

Respire with your partner at least seven long, deep breaths. It might be hard at first, but you'll have to hang it before long. If you and your partner enjoy the activity, do it – take 20 respirations together or 30 or only breathe together for a certain amount of time. There are no drawbacks to feel linked to your partner, so go for it!

This exercise will place you and your partner in an intimate and connected atmosphere. Practice it every time you feel the need to slow down and refocus.

4. Uninterrupted Listening

Another easy but strong practice, which sounds like it, is called uninterrupted listening. We just need to feel heard, respected and cared for, and both you and your partner should feel this way.

Set a timer (three to five minutes will normally go) for this exercise and encourage your partner to speak to you. They can talk about anything they want – work, school, you, kids, friends, family, stress – all of this is fair play.

Your job, as they talk, is to do only one thing: to listen. Don't talk until the timer is off. Just listen to your companion and take everything in. While you cannot speak during this time, you have the right to support or empathize your partner with your body language, facial expressions or meaningful looks without verbal words.

When the timer is off, change roles and begin the exercise again. One partner may be much more talking than the other, which is completely normal.

5. The Miracle Question

This exercise is a great way for couples to discuss how individually and as a couple, the future they want to create. We all aspire at times, but sometimes the battle is more complicated because we just don't know what our priorities really are – asking the "Miracle Question" will help you or your customers explain their goals.

This question allows all partners to test their own expectations and wishes and to learn about the dreams and desires of their partners. It will help a couple to realize what they and their other essential needs have to be fulfilled with their relationship.

Therapist Ryan Howes puts the miracle question like this:

"Suppose a miracle happened tonight while you slept. When you wake up tomorrow, what would you think will tell you that life got better suddenly? While both partners can provide a response that is unlikely in their waking lives, their answer can still be useful.

When the therapist performs pair therapy, he will delve into the unlikely dream of the consumer by asking: "How would that make a difference? This conversation helps the client to envisage a positive future for addressing or minimizing his or her issues and helps the therapist to understand how he or she can best serve their clients in the session. If you do that exercise without a therapist's help, do not try digging into the answer too deeply if it is impractical or difficult.

Use this conversation as an opportunity to learn about your partner and explore your future together.

6. The Weekly CEO Meeting

If you and your partner lead lives full of activities, events and responsibilities, this exercise is an excellent way to communicate.

This exercise helps you and your partner to communicate as an adult (no children allowed) and without interruption (no phones, tablets or laptops allowed).

Schedule a non-negotiable period of time (30 minutes is a reasonable amount) for you and your partner once a week to chat about how you and your partner are doing, your relationship as a pair, any unresolved disagreements or concerns, or any needs not met.

You can begin the exercise with questions such as:

How do you feel today about us?

Do you feel incomplete about something you'd like to talk about last week?

How can I make you feel more comfortable in the days ahead?

The answers to these questions should help you and your partner discuss yourself and your relationship in a safe and constructive way. Take care to keep up with any problems frequently and make sure things don't get swept under the rug or placed on the back burner for too long.

7. Five Things... Go! Exercise

This exercise can also be performed quickly and conveniently anytime the two of you are together. You just need your vocabulary and imagination!

Come and list five things in each category for every time you do this exercise-something like "what I am thankful for," "what I admire in you" or "what I want to do with you this month."

First, you can have a partner list all five things or, alternately, you and your partner can say one of your five things. But you choose to do it, be adventurous and don't be afraid to become dumb with your partner!

You might ask your partner, for example, "What five things do you love that I did lately for you? They might answer like, "Take out the trash, make a reservation for dinner, get thorough in my car, cuddle with me and watch my favorite film with me."

Once you have completed your list, please provide your own response to the question,

"Tell me how much you love me, picking up the weeds, putting the button back on my dress, kissing me every night."

You can chat about your things, show your appreciation to each other, ask questions or come together with more items when you've finished sharing your list.

This practice is a fun and engaging way to connect with your partner, to learn something new or to recall good memories.

CONCLUSION

I keep hearing the same question as my single friends and family members navigate the world of dating and finding love: Why do I still have the same kind of relation? "I started feeling hopeful about this relationship, but then everything fell apart like it always did, and the relationship wasn't going anywhere." "I thought it was a different time, but eventually it was crucial and rejection like my ex."

There's also an explanation for this enigmatic phenomenon? (Yes, there is.) Or are we actually scheduled to make the option of relationship? (In a way, yes, we are.) Our decisions are not mystical and so out of reach as we consider the attachment theory and its effect on us as children and adults. There are two fields of study on attachments. One studies the attachment patterns in romantically linked ties between child and caregiver; the other studies the attachment style of partners. They help us to understand our childhood attachment pattern and the attachment style that operates today in the romance of our relationships.

This may seem to be a lot of information to process, but it holds the key for the answers to why we continue to replicate the same destructive relationship habits irrespective of our best intentions. When we understand our childhood attachment patterns and adult attachment styles, we can change our conditioning by making new, healthier choices of partners. These acts would gradually weaken and replace the old memory traces of the brain. We will slowly change our attachment style and establish romantic ties based on a new and stable attachment style.

CPSIA information can be obtained
at www.ICGtesting.com
Printed in the USA
LVHW020942191020
669133LV00012B/507